Robert L. Goldman, PhD
Sanjib K. Mukherjee, MBA

Managed Service Restructuring in Health Care:
A Strategic Approach in a Competitive Environment

Pre-publication
REVIEWS,
COMMENTARIES,
EVALUATIONS . . .

"**T**his article is a breath of fresh air in the literature on reconfiguring health care. It combines strategic planning and produces differentiation paradigms with actual case studies. The authors appear to be experienced in working with hospitals faced with problems of integration of services in an intensely competitive environment and issues marking the move to TQM. This book has implications for integrated delivery systems. It combines macro-policy and micro-managerial perspectives."

Harold R. Hunter, MBA, PhD
Professor and Director,
Health Care Administration Program,
California State University,
Long Beach

More pre-publication
REVIEWS, COMMENTARIES, EVALUATIONS . . .

"**I**n an era of increasing pressure to achieve fiscal soundness of health care operations, decisions need to be made through a deliberate process that considers all alternatives. In their book, the authors offer a process centered on marketing financial analyses they call 'Managed Service Restructuring.'

This 'MSR' process, however, is more than just organized analytical steps. The authors present some candid and refreshing points of view. Since health care programs are important to their communities, for example, the establishment of a 'community advisory board' is recommended. And instead of just dropping a money-losing operation, the authors suggest 'harvesting' it–selling it to another operator so it continues to exist in the community. They also caution against 'an overeagerness to downsize.'

The strength of the book is its relevance to today's health care administrators, achieved primarily through dozens of examples and cases. These examples separate this book from the theoretical academic approach. They bring the text to life and should appeal to anyone involved in decision-making in today's challenging environment."

Christopher Orlie, MBA
President/CEO,
Hayes Orlie Cundall Inc.

"**I**n today's managed care environment, restructuring and positioning are matters of survival for health care entities. This book provides valuable insights and analytic tools for understanding and implementing the strategies required by the current trends in health care. Readers will learn several strategic methodologies for evaluating restructuring programs, and will understand the market implications of such decisions.

Chapter 2, 'MSR Defined,' identifies the warning signs of a program in crisis, explains the market and financial analyses required to use MSR in an effective manner, and provides a methodology to eliminate, enhance, or restructure the service and MSR options. Dr. Goldman poignantly exemplifies these principles with several case studies from around the country where MSR has been effectively used."

Steven Rousso, MBA
Senior Vice President,
HealthCare Financial Solutions

"**C**ontinuing and methodical change is described as an essential process in *Managed Service Restructuring in Health Care*. If an institution permits the process of change to be discontinuous, the organization, *de facto*, becomes reactionary to the environment in which it exists. This thesis is expounded by the authors, Goldman and Mukherjee, in a tight, almost outline, form. But the book provides a useful compass to those who accept the premises that are set forth. Arguably, the book is a disguised proposal for the value of external consultations to aid the processes of defining and implementing the periodic redesign and redeployment of a medical institution's resources and services.

The authors insist appropriately that changes of demands are persistent movements in an organization and its environments which will become disruptive, if not fatal, when they are not accepted as revolutionary forces that seek to modify erosion. If the forces are ignored, the restructuring is effected through convulsic modifications and probably revolutionary rearrangements. The book's content argues briefly and effectively for techniques that employ adequate data to inform the inevitable consequences of shifting societal demands for the delivery of medical care and health services."

Robert D. Sparks, MD
Vice President,
Howe-Lewis International, Inc.,
Menlo Park, California

The Haworth Press, Inc.

Managed Service Restructuring in Health Care
A Strategic Approach in a Competitive Environment

HAWORTH Marketing Resources
Innovations in Practice & Professional Services
William J. Winston, Senior Editor

New, Recent, and Forthcoming Titles:

Marketing Planning Guide by Robert E. Stevens, David L. Loudon, and William E. Warren

Marketing for Churches and Ministries by Robert E. Stevens and David L. Loudon

The Clinician's Guide to Managed Mental Health Care by Norman Winegar

Framework for Market-Based Hospital Pricing Decisions by Shahram Heshmat

Professional Services Marketing: Strategy and Tactics by F. G. Crane

A Guide to Preparing Cost-Effective Press Releases by Robert H. Loeffler

How to Create Interest-Evoking, Sales-Inducing, Non-Irritating Advertising by Walter Weir

Market Analysis: Assessing Your Business Opportunities by Robert E. Stevens, Philip K. Sherwood, and J. Paul Dunn

Selling Without Confrontation by Jack Greening

Persuasive Advertising for Entrepreneurs and Small Business Owners: How to Create More Effective Sales Messages by Jay P. Granat

Marketing Mental Health Services to Managed Care by Norman Winegar and John L. Bistline

New Product Screening: A Step-Wise Approach by William C. Lesch and David Rupert

Church and Ministry Strategic Planning: From Concept to Success by R. Henry Migliore, Robert E. Stevens, and David L. Loudon

Business in Mexico: Managerial Behavior, Protocol, and Etiquette by Candace Bancroft McKinniss and Arthur A. Natella

Managed Service Restructuring in Health Care: A Strategic Approach in a Competitive Environment by Robert L. Goldman and Sanjib K. Mukherjee

A Marketing Approach to Physician Recruitment by James Hacker, Don C. Dodson, and M. Thane Forthman

Marketing for CPAs, Accountants, and Tax Professionals edited by William J. Winston

Strategic Planning for Not-for-Profit Organizations by R. Henry Migliore, Robert E. Stevens, David L. Loudon, and Stan Williamson

Managed Service Restructuring in Health Care

A Strategic Approach in a Competitive Environment

Robert L. Goldman, PhD
Sanjib K. Mukherjee, MBA

Routledge
Taylor & Francis Group
New York London

First published 1995 by Haworth Press, Inc.

Published 2019 by Routledge
52 Vanderbilt Avenue, New York, NY 10017
2 Park Square, Milton Park, Abingdon, Oxon OX14 4RN

First issued in paperback 2019

Routledge is an imprint of the Taylor & Francis Group, an Informa business

Copyright © 1995 Taylor & Francis

Library of Congress Cataloging-in-Publication Data

Goldman, Robert, 1937-
 Managed service restructuring : a strategic approach in a competitive environment / Robert L. Goldman and Sanjib K. Mukherjee.
  p. cm.
 Includes bibliographical references and index.
 ISBN 1-56024-896-3 (acid-free paper)
 1. Managed care plans (Medical care)–Management. 2. Health services administration. 3. Corporate reorganizations. I. Mukherjee, Sanjib K. II. Title.
RA413.G59 1994
362.1′068–dc20   93-43876
                                                                                                                CIP

ISBN 13: 978-1-138-99553-6 (pbk)
ISBN 13: 978-1-56024-896-5 (hbk)

CONTENTS

ABOUT THE AUTHORS

Robert L. Goldman, PhD, is Senior Associate of the HealthCare Management Consortium, where his responsibilities include health care provider marketing management and consultation. A nationally recognized speaker, he has over 20 years of health care management and marketing experience. Dr. Goldman has published numerous articles on marketing, health care management, and managerial ethics, and is a member of the American Marketing Association and Northern California Health Care Executives.

Sanjib K. Mukherjee, MBA, DBA (cand.), is a management consultant. He has worked in management positions for companies in both service and product industries and has taught at college and university levels. Mr. Mukherjee's consulting and research has included the area of health care management, and he has published on managed service restructuring. He is currently a doctoral candidate in business administration.

ABOUT THE AUTHORS

Preface

Restructuring of a business often results in elimination of product lines and services, compelled either by dwindling earnings or motivated by the objective of increasing profits. Managed Service Restructuring (MSR) focuses on profitable but monitored organizational development to avoid unnecessary loss of services and jobs.

This book emphasizes MSR in relation to health care services. Particularly where people's health and welfare is at stake, we would hope that service restructuring is not an outcome of merely incompetent management and low profits.

Services and jobs can be gainfully continued in many instances of organizational restructuring. Management must understand the varying organizational needs in different stages of growth. Adequate and continual marketing and financial analyses, integrated into the business master plan, will facilitate MSR. We pursue these concepts in this book.

Relevant theories and practices pertaining to business development and MSR, coupled with practical case and situations analyses are included. We intend this book for health care administrators, educators, students, and interested readers. We thankfully acknowledge the suggestions of our friends who read parts of the manuscript and the assistance and patience of our editors.

Robert L. Goldman
Sanjib K. Mukherjee

Chapter 1

The Historical Basis
of Managed Service Restructuring

INTRODUCTION

To remain competitive and efficient, hospitals and other health service institutions must continually redefine themselves. This may mean introducing, eliminating, or otherwise modifying services. However, decisions are sometimes based on inadequate or faulty analytical techniques and erroneous assumptions.

Since the advent of the Prospective Payment System, hospitals have been forced to cut marginal services. Even when such a strategy is in conflict with the hospital's mission statement, service elimination often proceeds with the justification that the hospital must survive.

However, as health care continues to evolve toward an integrated, managed care system, the key players will need to make additional changes. The next decade will require the integration of financial analysis, market appraisal, and managerial skills. When price becomes less significant through managed care strategies, consumers will select providers based on quality and service.[1,2] This chapter explores the theoretical and analytical foundations for making successful restructuring decisions. It introduces Managed Services Restructuring (MSR), a deliberate and orchestrated management effort.

If the service must be eliminated, MSR provides the procedures that avoid last-ditch efforts to save an unsalvageable situation and are the least damaging to the institution and the public. Like products, services have life cycles and must be viewed differently as they move from one stage to the next. We begin the MSR analysis by reviewing the market position of the service based on product life cycle theory and related works. We then discuss several decision-making paradigms and finally examine actual situations in which the MSR approach has or could have been applied.

Goldman and Schore, in developing the concept of managed service restructuring, observed that the demand for acute hospital services is declining.[3] Advance planning, with simultaneous analysis of the financial and marketing elements of a service can avoid elimination of a potentially profitable service.

Such an analysis can be the basis of a realignment plan that can satisfy all publics: the community, the medical staff, the organization's employees, and its administrators. The worst time to make a restructuring decision is when a crisis arises. Thus, early detection of problems is critical.

THE PRODUCT LIFE CYCLE

Roberts offers another important element, stating that an organization must understand its position vis-à-vis the life span of each service it offers.[4] For example, hospitals may adopt new technology at different times in the product life cycle depending upon their mission or position.

Hospitals can be early adopters if they are research institutions or they may offer a service later in its life span if they are community hospitals. Thus, the MSR analysis of a service must take into account what type of hospital is being analyzed and where the service is in regard to its life span.

A review of the Product Life Cycle Theory and Portfolio Analysis will assist in understanding the MSR concept. Levitt describes four stages in the life of a product (or service) as shown in Figure 1:[5]

Stage 1: *Market Development* [Introduction]–This is when a new product is first brought to market, before there is a proven demand for it, and often before it has been fully proved out technically in all respects. Sales are low and creep along slowly.

Stage 2: *Market Growth*–Demand begins to accelerate and the size of the total market expands rapidly. It might also be called the "Takeoff Stage."

Stage 3: *Market Maturity*–Demand levels off and grows, for the most part, only at the replacement and new family-formation rate.

Stage 4: *Market Decline*–The product begins to lose consumer appeal and sales drift downward, such as when buggy whips lost out with the advent of automobiles and when silk lost out to nylon.[6]

Even in his early article on Product Life Cycle Theory, Levitt was looking at ways to modify the life of what the Boston Consulting Group (BCG) would later call the "Dogs." He showed that the decline stage may be delayed by one or more strategies including "Frequent Usage, Varied Usage, New Users and New Uses."[7]

THE PRODUCT LIFE CYCLE APPLIED TO HEALTH SERVICE ORGANIZATIONS

Starkweather and Kisch demonstrated that the life cycle may be modified within each industry.[8] Health services organizations pass through the following four phases:

Search: Characterized by newness, innovation and a sense of ascendancy as the organization proceeds to establish its identity. During this phase, the administrative structure is typically open and informal.

Success: During this phase, patients, staff, and resources are procured. The management becomes more formalized in order to handle a larger operation.

Bureaucratic: This phase is characterized by relatively rigid compliance to rules and procedures. The organization receives less feedback from its clients, creating an isolation. A decline may occur in this stage because of failure to respond to environmental changes.

Succession: New ways of providing services are developed often by the evolution of new units within the organization.

FIGURE 1: The Product Life Cycle

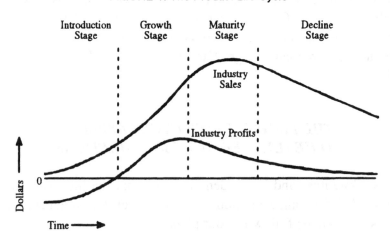

The need for restructuring can be prevented if the organization avoids moving into the Bureaucratic Phase. However, if this error cannot be avoided, then a need for service restructuring develops. The Succession Phase is when the restructuring of services and realignment of the organization takes place. Of course, this is the most costly way of rebuilding an organization.

PORTFOLIO ANALYSIS

A decade after Levitt's initial product life cycle work, Day and the BCG took a slightly different approach to product or service management.[9,10,11]

A diversified firm's operation is viewed in terms of a "portfolio of businesses." This technique categorizes different products or product lines in an organization's portfolio and determines optimal resource allocation.

This method has two determinants: an industry's growth rate and the relative market share of a firm's specific product(s). These reflect the product's competitive position and the net cash flow required to operate the business. The analysis involves a matrix divided into quadrants as shown in Figure 2.

The four categories are:

Rising Star:	High potential growth, modest (positive or negative) cash flow.
Cash Cow:	Large cash flow, modest or little growth.
Question Mark:[12]	Large, negative cash flow but high growth potential.
Dog:	Poor growth and cash flow.[13]

Since business units in each quadrant have different cash flow positions, they must be managed differently. This has an impact on the firm's overall operational strategy.

A later modification of The Boston Consulting Group's (BCG)

approach is known as the General Electric/McKinsey Business Assessment.[14] Porter states, "Depending on where a unit falls on the Company Position/Industry Attractiveness Screen Matrix, its broad strategic mandate is either to invest capital to *build* position, or to *harvest* or *divest*. Expected shifts in industry attractiveness or company position require reassessment of strategy."[15] Plotting a hospital's portfolio of businesses on such a matrix can help to ensure that the appropriate allocation of resources is made.

This approach requires a thorough analysis of each business unit, but does not consider remedial action. However, once a decision to divest is made, there is no opportunity for turnaround.

RESTRUCTURING MAY TAKE PLACE AT ALL LEVELS WITHIN AN ORGANIZATION

Leatt, Shortell, and Kimberly state that restructuring can affect the overall size of the organization as well as individual units.[16]

FIGURE 2: Growth/Share Matrix

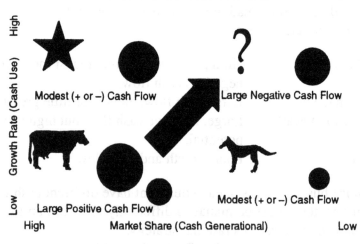

Business Assessment

It can also affect phasing out and/or shifting of managerial responsibility.

For example, a few years ago some surgical procedures, due to advances in technology and changes in reimbursement, were transferred from the classical in-patient surgical unit to a surgi-center. This required a change in management structure. In numerous cases a joint venture structure was developed with physicians that encouraged them to use the new surgi-center over one owned by a competing hospital. This response to competitive environmental forces was reasonable in the 1980s and worked relatively well. In the 1990s such situations would call for restructuring.

The recent change in the legal environment, i.e., changes in the Medicare Fraud and Abuse regulations, have placed traditional hospital-physician joint ventures in jeopardy. New ownership and management structures are being developed to respond to these changes.

Another significant change is moving from non-profit to for-profit status. While this change, on the surface, is limited to the organization's tax category, in reality it requires a radical change in the way management views itself. While we believe that today's nonprofits are as interested in capturing market share and improving the bottom line as any for-profits, there is still a difference in the types of funding mechanisms used and the justification for continuing services with weak demand.

Non-profit hospitals still provide charity care and solicit donations from the community to do so. A for-profit would find it difficult to attract contributions if the tax structure were known to potential donors because their contribution might not qualify as a charitable donation for tax purposes. In addition, a for-profit management team would probably be less hesitant to drop a service such as obstetrics when demand fell than a non-profit with a mission to serve the community. A management group, looking to retain community support, would take factors traditionally associated with nonprofit status even after the switch.

RESTRUCTURING FOR INCREASED PROFITABILITY

Scott and Shortell propose that profitable services should be reexamined periodically and upgraded or replaced if increased organizational effectiveness and efficiency would result.[17]

For example, a few years ago a 300-bed community hospital operated by a religious organization in the San Francisco Bay Area, was in an enviable position. It had an occupancy rate over 90 percent and was adding a new member to its medical staff on a daily basis. Still, the director of planning and marketing reviewed all services routinely. She knew two facts: (1) markets change and the hospital could see a downturn in business, and (2) the hospital must make a profit in order to fulfill its religious obligation of service to the community.

Over a three-year period, she restructured two services by combining them and eliminated another. To use a phrase from the life insurance industry, she "Traded Up" and increased the effectiveness, efficiency, and profit per bed. To Trade Up is to reduce or eliminate low-profit clients for customers who buy more or are more profitable. For example, reducing Medicaid admissions in favor of private insurance patients would be considered Trading Up. In this case the director eliminated a service that was not vital to the community and captured new patients by combining the two other units into a more efficient and attractive structure. This permitted her hospital to provide better charity care.

THE BASIS FOR FUTURE ANALYSIS

Each of these historical approaches has aided in the development of the MSR approach. The relationship of the service to its stage of the life cycle determines appropriate pricing, access and distribution, and promotion.

The BCG category gives an indication of how well resources have been allocated and how they may be reallocated in the future, while the business assessment approach helps managers to determine future strategies. The specific industry, be it health care or another, and the tax status, i.e., not-for-profit or for-profit, also play significant roles.

A profitable and useful service may also be restructured in order to increase its competitiveness and profitability. However, none of these elements is of value unless the financial and marketing analyses are performed concurrently and accurately.

OBJECTIVE OF THIS BOOK

We are attempting to provide you with a solid theoretical base for what we have developed into MSR. In addition, we want to prepare you for implementing MSR techniques by describing them in sufficient detail for your application to your own situation and also by offering examples of when and how they have been applied. We also include some horror stories about situations that could have had positive outcomes if only people had listened to us.

In Chapter 2 we define MSR. We state that it is a conscious management effort and not a crisis management tool. By this we mean that the MSR approach should be included in your organization's strategic plan. MSR can be a preventive instrument as well as one that saves lives.

We offer you a set of warning signals that should alert you to the need to review the services and/or products offered. Of course, decreased utilization is one indicator. Another is a decline in revenue or utilization in related services. You might also consider a review when the number of FTEs (Full Time Equivalents) required to maintain revenue and/or the amount of promotional funds needed increases. Keeping in touch with demographic changes in your community is also important.

You will also find a discussion of the utility of MSR techniques in this chapter. We believe that the MSR approach will help channel scarce resources to the services the community wants and needs the most. In turn, this will improve the viability of your organization.

We caution against an overeagerness to downsize. Without critical mass, an institutional provider will lose the loyalty of the medical staff, its best employees, and the support of the community. The MSR approach can guide you to a program that should be restructured by any one of the three approaches known: harvest, divest, and build. Too many hospitals and other health care organizations have become "Infinitely Efficient." That is, they have cut costs to zero by going out of business.

A facility that has chosen to defer maintenance to more profitable times will not survive until those times come. In fact, downsizing may increase the rate of decline as your best people realize what the outcome is probably going to be. One can stand at the helm and complain about rats leaving a sinking ship, but these people are not rats: they usually are your most competent employees and most active members of your medical staff. They leave because they have other places to go and you are left with marginal people.

In this chapter, we also discuss a management principle that is often neglected. That is, "Don't make enemies by accident." There are times when you must divest yourself of a popular but under-used service. The process is as important as the decision.

By involving your communities through advisory boards and open hearings you may find that people will come around to your point of view. They may not like what you must do, but they will understand your reasoning.

You may also find that you have supporters you did not realize you had and that they may come up with creative solutions to your problem. At worst, you will have gained acceptance without having to sacrifice a valued administrator to an unsympathetic and demanding public.

We next attempt to spell out the techniques involved in the MSR approach. There are two different analyses involved. One is from a marketing point of view and the other takes a financial approach.

All too often one or the other analysis is overlooked because of the person conducting the review and that person's background. Both aspects are essential. We have seen situations in which expenses but not revenues were allocated to a service to reduce inpatient utilization in a managed care environment. This decimated the outpatient portion of the service and lost profitable customers.

The two must be blended into a management report that provides a thorough review of the current situation and an analysis of *all reasonable* alternatives. Too often this type of report becomes a sales tool for a single point of view. Because the objective of the report is to sell a previously determined point of view, community boards and medical staff review task forces as well as employees affected by the decision, who can easily see through such a subterfuge.

When the decision is made to harvest, divest, or build, a complete action is necessary. We offer a set of steps within each plan designed to help you achieve your goal as painlessly as possible. Divestiture does not mean that the service will no longer be offered or that you will lose all of your investment in it. You may find another organization that has been competing with you that could use your remaining client base and other resources.

Even a harvested service may remain a part of a more viable unit serving a limited population with reduced costs. It will also be possible to develop a program that will cost-effectively build a program. A restructuring of management, staffing, and promotion may turn what looks like a dog into a rising star.

A final point within Chapter 2 is a reminder that communities must be served. We look at the ethical consequences of cutting off a service from a profit-oriented point of view. We suggest that MSR techniques may help you escape this trap.

In Chapter 3 we discuss how to apply the MSR approach. First, there must be involvement and commitment from senior management. Since the analysis is new and has a cost attached to it, this may be hard to obtain. The approach can be performed in a short period of time by qualified staff members, but it will take longer than an *ad hoc* staff meeting in which the CEO demands and gets a simple solution to a complex problem.

Internal management needs to support the concept that restructuring decisions affect all communities that your organization comes in contact with. Mid-level and senior people need to see that your organization is unitary in nature and that a decision made in one area has significant and often adverse consequences in another.

Since the MSR approach calls for a new point of view and the application of techniques are new or in a new format, you may find that outside consultants can be of use. This chapter suggests criteria and a process by which you can meet your needs without unnecessary expense. As each new management technique comes to market, a growing number of people will attempt to conquer it for their own gain. Some will master it and some will master how to market themselves with little value to their clients. We will also recommend how to develop your own expertise in order to reduce consultations or interact more effectively with your outside experts.

This chapter also covers how to reduce or eliminate operational bias. Health services managers are under a high degree of pressure to cut expenses in order to improve profitability. Often they must make decisions rapidly and with limited data. We hope that our approach will reduce this practice.

Operational bias can be reduced by involving the medical staff and community leaders. We discuss specific methods to accomplish this while maintaining control within your administration.

One method used to build or rebuild a service is to develop a joint venture with other providers to offer the service. We discuss complications to avoid and also show how joint ventures can work. Your attorney must be brought into the process at the earliest point and familiarized about the MSR approach.

You will often find that you will have to work with your

competitors to continue to serve the community. We address the issues and methods involved to successfully work together.

We are also going into detail in regard to employee concerns and cooperation. We believe that it is best to keep everyone informed as fully as possible. We also suggest a set of ground rules if information must be kept confidential and urge that they be shared with everyone involved before the situation comes up.

The last section of Chapter 3 is a discussion of how to develop and implement the operational plan. We suggest that you review all elements of your business plan to see how the new blueprint should be integrated into the existing one. We recommend ways to keep everyone informed as you make progress toward increased profitability and service.

In Chapter 4 we discuss using the MSR approach to prevent service line deterioration. We recommend that all service lines be reviewed periodically. We suggest how senior administrators and planners can assist in the process by offering an analysis of the external environments that all can use. This reduces the potential for developing objectives based on different sets of data.

We advise that the MSR approach be applied before new services are developed. We have seen situations in which needed and potentially profitable services are irrevocably damaged because one or more groups have not been brought into the planning process. We also discuss how to avoid overoptimistic marketing and financial projections by using forecasting techniques that give you a reasonable level of accuracy.

Since the "Center(s) of Excellence" concept is often at the heart of attempts to develop new markets, we include a section in this chapter on how to build such a center while avoiding common errors.

Again, senior management is reviewed because of the need for them to accept responsibility and accountability for the process and its outcomes. One major reason that the process fails is that no single person is in charge. New services have a high mortality rate because of external factors. Thus, it is wasteful to begin to develop something new if there is no political support. One way to ensure support is to assign a senior manager to be in charge of all aspects of the project.

We believe that the MSR approach can be used to encourage innovation at all levels, which is also discussed in this chapter. The MSR approach permits people to take risks by reducing the number of unknowns involved in starting a new service. Because everyone involved has the same information and can share their assumptions, misinformation is reduced. Also, since the process is part of the strategic planning review, few surprises arise to cause problems. We also look at one problem with total quality management (TQM); it requires employees to work at their optimal level.

We offer a modification that we call LCD/Fail-Safe to ensure that customers receive the best service possible. A guiding principle is developed for each critical factor for success and all employees are empowered to make decisions.

The final section of this chapter discusses our conclusions and recommendations. We restate the basic concepts involved in the MSR approach and show how a new program can be developed.

Chapter 5 is a series of cases in which the MSR approach has been used or could have been used.

HOW YOU SHOULD BENEFIT FROM THIS BOOK

You will probably sleep better because of this book. We have tested it on several hundred health services managers and found that their mean-time to slumber was decreased by 92 percent on the first night. You may also find that the MSR approach and the tools we offer you will reduce both internal and external conflict at your health care organization.

While many of the examples take place within acute care hospitals, the MSR approach and this book is designed to assist any health care administrator or manager.

As CEO, you might find that the MSR approach will extend your contract because you will have fewer conflicts with the medical staff. Our recent research confirms the conclusions of many others, that CEO retention beyond three years is iffy at best and often dependent on maintaining good relations with the medical staff.

As CEO, you should consider this book as a tool to provide you with a fresh approach to dealing with those irrational marketing people down the hall. You will see that Finance and Marketing must work together for the MSR approach to succeed and that when they do the organization benefits from increased efficiency and effectiveness.

As Vice-President of Patient Care Services, you will have a new approach to stabilize your staff and to support you when you see an orphan service that is important to the community.

As Chief Information Officer, you will be able to better provide the data and systems needed within this improved decision-making process.

As Chief Marketing Officer, you will have a new tool to convert the traditionalists to your point of view that marketing is essential to organizational success. You will be able to demonstrate that the 4Ps of marketing are not Promotion, Promotion, Promotion, and Promotion. The planning process will flow more smoothly with the MSR approach in place.

REFERENCE NOTES

1. Joyce Jensen, "Consumers Consider Quality in Deciding on a Hospital, but Measurements Differ," *Modern Healthcare*, March 10, 1989, p. 86.

2. Chip R. Bell & Ron Zemke, "Commitment to Service is Good Strategy," *Hospitals*, May 5, 1991, p. 56.

3. Robert L. Goldman & Jean E. Schore, "Managed Service Restructuring: When The Market Changes, Everyone Can Still Win," *Hospital Strategy Report*, Volume 1, Number 10, August, 1989.

4. Robert D. Roberts, "ROTEC Theory: Planning Tool to Position Hospitals on the Technology Curve," *Hospital Strategy Report*, Volume 2, Number 8, June, 1990.

5. Theodore Levitt, "Exploit the Product Life Cycle," *Harvard Business Review*, Volume 43, Number 6, November/December, 1965, pp. 81 ff.

6. *Ibid.*, p. 81.

7. *Ibid.*, p. 89.

8. D. B. Starkweather & A. I. Kisch, "A Model of the Life Cycle Dynamics of Health Science Organizations." Originally cited in M. Arnold, L.V. Blankenskip & J. M. Hess, Eds., *Administering Health Systems*, Aldine-Atherton Press, Chicago, 1971. Discussed in Stephen M. Shortell & Arnold D. Kaluzny, *Health Care Management: A Text in Organization Theory and Behavior*, 2nd. Ed., Wiley, New York, 1988, p. 329.

9. Bruce D. Henderson, *Henderson on Corporate Strategy*, Abt Books, 1979, p. 24 ff.

10. George S. Day, "Diagnosing the Product Portfolio," *Journal of Marketing*, April, 1977, p. 31 ff. See also John S. Hammond & Gerald B. Allan, "A Note on the Boston Consulting Group Concept of Competitive Analysis and Corporate Strategy," HBS Case Services No. 175-175.

11. Bruce Henderson, *The Logic of Business Strategy*, Ballinger, Cambridge, MA, 1984, p. 58.

12. Also known as a "Problem Child."

13. George S. Yip, "Market Selection and Direction: Role of Product Portfolio Planning," *Harvard Business Review*, Reprint 581-107, 1981.

14. Michael E. Porter, *Competitive Strategy: Techniques for Analyzing Industries and Competitors*, The Free Press, New York, 1980, p. 365.

15. *Ibid.*

16. Peggy Leatt, Stephen M. Shortell & John R. Kimberly, "Chapter 9: Organization," within Shortell & Kaluzny, *op. cit.*, p. 309.

17. W. Richard Scott & Stephen M. Shortell, "Chapter 12: Organizational Performance: Managing for Efficiency and Effectiveness," in Shortell & Kaluzny, *op.cit.*, pp. 418-419.

Chapter 2

MSR Defined

A CONSCIOUS MANAGEMENT EFFORT

Managed Service Restructuring is a process that permits managers to afford a service its maximum possible productivity within the overall marketing effort of the organization. MSR may involve a conscious management effort to retain a seemingly unprofitable existing service. The service may appear to be unprofitable for either the short- or long-run. The need for MSR may arise either because of changes in demands or because of inadequate management.

WARNING SIGNS

The symptoms that indicate an impending crisis include:

- the demand for the service is declining at an increasing rate,
- maintaining the current level of revenue requires an increase in promotional activities,
- the number of employees per unit of service is rising,
- related services are also experiencing one or more of the above symptoms, and/or
- demographic or competitive changes that result in these symptoms.[1]

THE UTILITY OF MSR

The MSR technique is most profitably used when management is unable to identify the stages of a service's life cycle, or to recognize its place in the organization's portfolio.

However, the contention in this book is that MSR be considered in all situations involving the possibility of any service elimination.

The basis for this contention is that:[2]

1. health service involves public service; service discontinuation affects the health and welfare of human beings,
2. restructuring involves analyses to determine whether a profitable means of salvaging the service exists and allows the institution to re-evaluate its financial and marketing strategies,[3] and
3. restructuring safeguards against elimination because of erroneous assumptions and theoretical bias.[4]

AN OVEREAGERNESS TO DOWNSIZE

Greene reviewed studies in which health care institutions, faced with the option of downsizing or eliminating parts of their portfolios, have seen friction between administrators and the hospital's publics such as: the community, employees, the medical staff, the media, etc.[5] Often, the institution's managers wanted to eliminate the service while consultants hired to review the situation advocated retention.

In a study that has value in the health care delivery system, Hambrick and MacMillan studied the performance of over 1,000 industrial products and found that, on the average, products designated as Dogs maintained positive cash flows.[6]

Downsizing May Increase the Decline

Henkoj states that downsizing may, in fact, damage the organization.[7] "Downsizing has become an opiate for many companies."[8] He advocates the position, stated by Greenberg that, "downsizing begets more downsizing."[9] Downsizing is bad because it affects morale, reduces initiative, and affects quality of work.

Greene has noted that many managers equate elimination with failure caused by "poor planning, poor implementation or poor management."[10] Often the "exit policies" occur because of "analysis paralysis."

DO NOT MAKE ENEMIES BY ACCIDENT

Rather than using downsizing as a strategy, one can apply the MSR technique. One important principle is to *not make enemies by accident.* That is, the course of action to be taken should regard the needs and sensibilities of the hospital's publics. Jensen cites an NRC study that shows that people are willing to pay more for personal attention and quality service rather than make a random selection of providers.[11] Thus, a strategy of providing high quality will maintain sound relations with a provider's client base.

MSR TECHNIQUES

First, carry out analyses of the financial and market factors and establish whether the service is in fact a "Dog." If analyzing a product or service suggests it is a "Dog" or in the decline stage, the service may have to be eliminated. However, managers should also consider "harvesting" (selling off a service to another organization) or modifying the way the service is offered.

These analyses are followed by the blending of the two into a management report that evaluates all reasonable options. If the alternative selected is to eliminate the service, then a specific set of activities is developed that anticipates the response of each segment of the community.

THE MARKETING ANALYSIS

This analysis begins with a review of the current situation within the organization in relation to the environment in which it operates. The mission statement or business definition must correlate with the reality of how the organization operates. This definition must be narrow enough to focus the organization so that resources are not wasted, but also wide enough to ensure that opportunities are not missed.

Problems develop when the financial need to be cost-effective (the need to increase profits) conflicts with organizational needs to meet charitable objectives. For example, one religious-based not-for-profit hospital had a business definition of service to all regardless of ability to pay. However, its operational plan stated a goal of reducing Medicaid and charity care to 15 percent. The mission statement had not been reviewed when the new business plan was written.

This type of incongruence leads to confusion within the organization, mixed signals to the community, and a wasting of resources as enemies are made by accident. Following review of the business definition, the marketing goals of the organization should be defined for the short-range and long-range periods out to about five years. (Note: within the overall business plan the marketing, financial, and operational goals will all be presented.)

Long-range goals are intended to guide the organization but not restrain it. Those involved in the process should expect that these goals will change as the environment changes.

The next section is a situation or environmental analysis often called a SWOT Analysis. SWOT is an acronym for *S*trengths, *W*eaknesses, *O*pportunities and *T*hreats. A review of the organization's internal resources is the first step. These of course include financial and human resources. But other items are also incorporated such as patents, unique operational abilities, networking relationships, and the reputation in the community. A Center of Excellence may offer a halo effect that creates a better image of the entire organization, for example.

Often, special talents are overlooked or taken for granted. A team of nurses, for example, who have extraordinary abilities to maintain low infection rates may go unnoticed unless a thorough analysis is completed.

One 250-bed community hospital had a volunteer who combined two unique attributes into a fund-raising effort that raised over $100,000 per year. He was an avid golfer who worked in the airline industry. This led to an annual golf tournament that attracted senior executives throughout the airline industry.

The external world is divided into several environments to make it easier to understand and also to remind us to consider all factors.

One element is the competitive environment. We want to know who our competitors are, how well they are doing, and what changes they are contemplating. This is easier than it sounds and does not require industrial espionage.

Hospital statistics are easy to obtain from state or industry sources. Publicity releases often give insight into future plans and keeping one's eyes and ears open also helps. The basic maxim is that you have one mouth and two ears and should use them in that ratio. Let the other organization's people brag while you keep your plans as quiet as possible. Human nature is such that most competitors will disclose much more than necessary.

Another tool sounds a bit like wool-gathering but is very useful. It might be called informal gaming. You start with the question, "If I were running their surgi-center, what would I do?" By placing yourself in your competition's situation, you will often find that you can predict their actions. One of the authors (Goldman) has been involved in gaming on several occasions. One time a change in employment from one organization to another permitted a look at the business plan of the new employer. The results were very close to the projections made during the author's previous employment. Remember, your competitor should also be using this technique and may anticipate your tactical or strategic initiatives.

The political/legal environment changes rapidly within health care. Structures and activities that were logical and practical yesterday may no longer be permitted today.[12]

Physician-owned laboratories are an example of changes that are both a threat and an opportunity. Since self-referral is no longer an accepted promotional strategy because of Medicare Fraud and Abuse regulations, an outside organization may be able to gain entrance into a new market by buying out the physician owners since the new organization would be developed on a sound business basis and would not self-deal. (Note: the authors believe that self-referral at best is sloppy marketing. Hospitals that set-up hospital-physician joint ventures for the sole purpose of obtaining new business from these doctors usually find that the venture is full of problems.)[13]

The economic environment often is affected by the political/legal environment. Changes in government-based reimbursement are precursors to changes in the private sector. Providers who fail to take these changes into account will no longer be competitive. But administrators must also stay on top of the local economic situation and trends–the micro-environment. As "Managed Competition" is considered to control health care costs, for example, administrators will have to develop strategies not only within their primary market but also at the regional level where prices may be set.

The technological environment also changes rapidly in health care. While we are aware of swift changes in medical technology and their effects on the capital budget, there are other technological changes that affect our overall efforts.

Advances in Health Information Systems (HIS), for example, can be the basis of hospital-physician linkages that make it easier for doctors with multiple hospital affiliations to practice at one hospital over another. If one hospital develops a local area network that ties physician offices to each other and the hospital, a doctor within the network will find that it is easier to order a consult or obtain current lab values for patients admitted to that hospital compared to one not in the system.

Today's effective HIS also provides more useful data than ever before. A community needs analysis can be more thorough and accurate because of the ability to use your HIS to manipulate demographic data such as birth rates, income distribution, education levels, and other related elements that can help you develop a profile of your community.

The social/cultural environment also presents opportunities and threats. Wellness programs, as an example, that have been poorly received in the past are now being accepted without backlash.[14] Another change that must be considered is the aging of America. The baby boomers are now moving into middle age. (You knew it had to happen.) Coupled with the influx of young immigrants, many health care organizations are faced with the necessity to provide care to two very different groups since these market segments have dissimilar needs.

While the older group is subject to chronic problems such as diabetes or heart disease, the younger group is most affected by infections and trauma. Another factor is that the two groups seem to have different values and expectations from their health care providers. The older group might expect, "The best that money can buy," while the younger people might not anticipate receiving more than minimal care.

Once the SWOT analysis has been completed and validated, specific objectives may be developed. These objectives attempt to provide measurable benchmarks by which your efforts can be evaluated as you try to reach your marketing goals.

A mid-range goal might be to achieve a 15 percent market share in the outpatient physical therapy segment over the next three years. One objective designed to help the organization meet this goal might be the development of an occupational medicine program.

In completing the marketing analysis, care should be given to develop an understanding of the evaluation process. Each evaluation technique should be analyzed to determine its reliability, validity, and appropriateness to your particular situation. You must start with baseline historical data so that you can determine whether the changes you make have an effect.

Surveys to determine use or awareness, focus groups that are designed to elicit feelings and knowledge, coupons, advertisements with different response telephone numbers, or identification codes are a few of the evaluation tools available to you. The principle should be that all marketing efforts should have an appropriate evaluation component. Unless you assign a person to be responsible for the evaluation process and include it in your marketing budget, you are wasting resources.

THE FINANCIAL ANALYSIS

The financial analysis needs to include both costs and revenues if it is to be valid and useful. An example of what not to do is right on point. One hospital CFO muddied the picture by trying to reduce inpatient physical therapy for patients covered by managed care contracts. He allocated expenses but not a portion of the *per diem* charges or global payments.

The CFO reasoned that he could minimize the service provided by showing that it was a cost center instead of a revenue center. He hoped that the amount of service per patient would decrease with the effect of increasing his profit margin on these patients. He was wrong.

Needed capital equipment was not purchased. Physicians continued to prescribe physical therapy to these patients based on needs and not on the cost/revenue allocation. The result was that service quality deteriorated, hard-to-recruit physical therapists left the institution, and highly profitable outpatient physical therapy declined.

While this example was a relatively simple predicament, the usual circumstances are harder to analyze. The Emergency Department is often a typical situation.

Many hospitals receive 20 to 50 percent of their admissions through the emergency department. Numerous administrators have been taught that the emergency department is a loss-leader but essential to the hospital. While it may be essential it may not have to be a loss-leader.

Two strategies may change the situation. First, the cost allocation method should reflect the direct costs of the department and its contribution to fixed costs and profit. While it may sound very basic, costs that are not attributable to the department should be excised from its budget.

Second, a contract with a group of emergency medicine physicians may include all the personnel in the department. With the correct contract structure and reasonable incentives, the department can become a revenue center.

In summary, the financial analysis should reflect actual revenues and expenses and should not be used as a punitive measure. With an effective HIS, management can incorporate significant financial information into management decisions.

BLENDING THE TWO TO DEVELOP A MANAGEMENT REPORT

The management report should analyze all reasonable alternatives in order to permit a rational choice. One should not develop a forced choice process but include relevant information about all alternatives–not solely the one you want to see accepted. It is essential to include the medical staff in the decision-making process.

In addition to background data, you need to include a set of criteria that describes an ideal situation. These criteria would characterize the use of resources and the outcomes of your actions. Thus, you generate a method of testing your alternatives. You can expect to see them modified as the process continues.

Once the alternatives have been evaluated, you are prepared to commit to the one with the highest probability of success and acceptance. If your choice is to eliminate the service, you must take special steps to reduce or abrogate adverse consequences. This is discussed in the next section.

Regardless of what strategy you choose, you will find it essential to develop a set of tactics and activities to move the process forward. You will need to look at more than the product or service under review. You will have to discern its effects on other services, how changes in pricing, distribution, or promotion will alter the entire organizational effort as well as the effect these changes will have on your community. You will see that each element in the marketing mix, that is, product, price, place, and promotion, includes the potential for strategies that can overcome weaknesses found in other areas. For example, a low-priced competitor may be surmounted with an enhanced product.

ELIMINATING THE SERVICE

If the service must be eliminated, the community should be brought into the decision-making process, through the development of a community advisory board, surveys, or any other methods that acknowledge public opinion, so that they accept the course of action. They will not be happy about the loss of a valued service, but they will have little or no animosity toward the institution or the decision makers.

The development of a community advisory board and the holding of community meetings to explain the problem and listen to alternatives can build goodwill. Of course, an open mind is essential. Ground rules need to be stated. The community members are more likely to accept the concept that change must occur in order to maintain the overall health of the institution.

A community advisory board can be an excellent source of information and ideas. It must be managed carefully so that the members feel that they are part of the process and not there to merely endorse decisions made by others.

The same principle holds true when other segments are involved such as nurses, other employees, or physicians. Two critical axia should be followed: do not make enemies by accident, and remember that we all have special knowledge but are also ignorant of what others know.

Those people who are the most valuable are also the busiest. Physicians in private practice, serving on hospital committees, usually do not want to attend meetings. Their volunteer efforts must result in a perceived value to them.

HARVESTING THE SERVICE

The service may be transferred or sold off to a competitor. One reason for doing so is that a complete analysis may find that the service in question is declining because a competitor is increasing market share.

A competitor may be willing and capable of ensuring the continuity of the service.[15] By working with your community leaders and the competitor who will continue the service, you will have an opportunity to build goodwill while cutting costs.

INTERNAL RESTRUCTURING OF THE SERVICE

The service may also be restructured or rebuilt within the organization. It may be moved from an inpatient to an outpatient setting.[16] The number of employees may be reduced. The location may be changed. Promotion can be increased, reorganized, or reduced. Pricing may also be realigned. The objective, under this option, is to increase usage or users as Levitt recommended.[17] It is also possible to merge two units providing similar or complementary services. A joint-venture with another institution, or with members of the medical staff, is also an alternative.

One example occurred when two San Francisco Bay Area hospitals, about three miles apart, merged their psychiatric units. One hospital had a closed unit while the other had an open ward.

The two units were complementary. While there was some competition between them, they were complementary in nature since the medical staffs overlapped while the patient base was different. Both units were underutilized.

The merger of the open ward with the closed unit resulted in administrative savings. The nursing staff was reduced through attrition and lay-offs were avoided. The unit is significantly stronger than its predecessors.

While this example demonstrates how MSR techniques can be applied in a routine situation, another example shows how they may be applied to avoid making enemies by accident. In the following example, the two units were *not* merged.

One hospital, located in the Bay Area and a leader in its community, provides physical therapy through an outpatient unit that competes with its own sports medicine center. Each service owns its own equipment and is operated by separate administrative teams. In addition, there is no cooperative marketing. Such a situation appears to be highly wasteful. However, the two units target different markets.

The sports medicine center is described as a center of excellence developed by the hospital because of the personal interest of one physician. The equipment is of a better quality than the outpatient unit and there is more of it.

Both units provide a high level of service to their patients. However, the outpatient unit's patients have routine problems such as on-the-job injuries, strokes, and broken hips while the sports medicine center's patients are young and healthy. Many come from professional sports.

The physician in charge of the sports medicine unit objects when the issue of a merger is raised, and rightly so. The sports medicine center would lose patients if merged with the other unit. Its identity would be lost. Sports medicine is often a high-risk venture. A separate identity is essential to success. The market analysis demonstrated that the option with the highest probability of success would be the separate unit.

Each situation must be analyzed on its own merits. Sheldon S. King of Cedars-Sinai Medical Center of Los Angeles found it beneficial to cooperate with UCLA Medical Center to avoid unnecessary competition, thereby serving the region more appropriately with only services that the centers are best at providing.[18]

King also stated that hospitals should go beyond health care and provide services to the community such as access to proper housing, adequate nutrition, and counseling after discharge from the hospital. Thus, Mr. King enhanced the services offered by both institutions and also improved service to the community by using the equivalent of MSR techniques.

Another example comes from Torrance, California. The Torrance Memorial Medical Center divested itself of four of its major out-patient services to a for-profit joint venture with its medical staff.

The new entity, Health Access Systems, averted competition from members of the medical staff, expanded market share, increased revenue, and built a well-capitalized base for further ventures. By providing more than one service, the new corporation had a major competitive advantage.[19]

Since each provider operates in a unique environment, there

cannot be a formula that is applicable to all. The MSR approach depends upon dual analyses that provide a complete picture of the provider's problems and opportunities.

All too often, we hear administrators complain that they attempted to implement one marketing technique or another without success. Often the phrase is, "We tried it once and it didn't work."

As with other marketing tools, the MSR techniques will only work if the analyses are based on sound research and the application is managed by creative and experienced professionals.

MSR OPTIONS

As a broad and general guideline, MSR may be applied as follows:

Options	Conditions
1. Selling off	All other options considered inappropriate.
2. Selling off to a competitor	Dwindling demand is the result of the rising market share of the competitor and the organization is unable to regain market share.
3. Rebuild within the organization	Product life cycle and status of the service identified, restructuring found feasible based on marketing and financial analyses.
4. Joint-venture	Restructuring needed because a new source of financing and expertise are required.

Even though the pressure on the health service institutions to cut costs, either by eliminating services or downsizing operations, is today's health care environment, some administrators are inherently inclined toward elimination of services and scaling down of operations based on their belief that profitability is their sole objective.

COMMUNITIES MUST CONTINUE TO BE SERVED

In opposition to this contention, many health services professionals believe that services should be continued even if unprofitable, as long as the institution can support it from Cash Cows. They argue that service to the community should come before profits.[20,21]

The reality is that administrators must show results rapidly or face the loss of their jobs. A recent survey conducted by the authors showed that over 47 percent of Bay Area administrators of community hospitals (excluding HMO facilities) had held their positions for three years or less. However, another 30 percent had retained their jobs for over seven years.

This bi-modal distribution may be caused by the approaches used by these administrators. The CEOs with short tenure have attempted to increase profitability through cost-cutting. This technique has its limits. Once every bit of fat has been cut out and reductions are still needed to show a profit, or at least break even, this type of administrator is out of ideas and often out of a job.

CEOs with longer terms have learned that expansion of services and increased market share are also essential. They understand their markets and are alerted to changes through ongoing research. The complacent administrator no longer exists. There are only narrow thinkers who depend on cost cutting and strategic visionaries who are attuned to their communities.

An excellent example of this point comes from a county hospital. Lutz discusses North Mississippi Medical Center.[22] The hospital was able to justify an expansion that included 75 beds, a $6 million diagnostic imaging center, a 124-bed women's hospital, a free-standing surgical center, and an off-site warehouse. While many rural hospitals are downsizing and county hospitals often are in financial trouble, North Mississippi Medical Center is profitable. The administrator, John D. Hicks, took a creative approach by reframing his hospital as a private not-for-profit. He developed the nation's first rural referral center, a designation that includes higher Medicare reimbursement, and retained support of the community by promising county officials that he would continue to serve the county's patients.[23]

North Mississippi Medical Center is now a network of seven rural hospitals that serve 22 counties. Because of its new structure, it is more diversified. Sixty beds have been converted to skilled nursing. Of the 650,000 people it serves, about 68 percent of the patients come from outside the county.[24] The restructuring has converted a 1950s traditional hospital into a modern health care center that meets the needs of its communities in the 1990s.

Regardless of the approach to be used, optimal results require both a financial and a marketing analysis as well as a reasonable plan and input from all segments of the community. The decision to build, harvest, or divest will be much easier to make under these circumstances. You will find that the MSR approach will help you retain community respect and, perhaps, your job.

REFERENCE NOTES

1. Robert L. Goldman & Jean E. Schore, "Managed Service Restructuring," *HealthCare Productivity Report*, Volume 2, Number 9, September, 1989.

2. Robert L. Goldman & Sanjib K. Mukherjee (name omitted from original article, correction made in the Winter, 1992, Vol. XI, No. 3), "Managed Service Restructuring: A Brief Analysis," *Central Business Review*, Summer, 1992, Vol. XI, No. 3, p. 32.

3. This, in turn, enables the institution to recognize and rectify past failures that have led to the crisis.

4. For example: the service appears to be unprofitable and must be eliminated without consideration of the effect on other services.

5. Jay Greene, "A Strategy for Cutting Back," *Modern Healthcare*, August 18, 1989, p. 29 ff.

6. Donald C. Hambrick & Ian C. MacMillan, "The Product Portfolio and Man's Best Friend," *California Management Review*, Volume 25, Number 1, pp. 84-85.

7. Ronald Henkoj, "Cost Cutting: How to Do It Right," *Fortune*, April 9, 1990, p. 40 ff.

8. *Ibid.*, p. 40

9. Eric Greenberg, Editor, *The American Management Association Research Reports*, cited by Henkoj, p. 40.

10. Greene, *op. cit.*, pp. 30, 38.

11. Jensen, *op. cit.*, p. 90.

12. For a further discussion of the environments in which we compete and barriers to entry into a market, see: Michael E. Porter, "Chapter 2: How Competitive Forces Shape Strategy," Cynthia A. Montgomery & Michael E. Porter, Eds., *Strategy: Seeking and Securing Competitive Advantage*, Harvard Business Review, Boston, 1991, pp. 11-25.

13. See Robert L. Goldman, John H. Jackson & Claire B. Shoen, "Physician-Hospital Joint Ventures: Issues, Risks and Benefits," *Journal of Hospital Marketing*, Vol. 3(1), 1988, p. 9 ff.

14. Julie Johnson, "Wellness Efforts: Hospitals Boost Education, Awareness—Without Physician Backlash," *Hospitals*, April 20, 1992, pp. 46-49.

15. Antitrust laws must be reviewed to ensure that no illegal division of markets is contemplated.

16. See Roberts, *op. cit.* for a discussion of moving a service based on the technology curve.

17. Levitt, *op. cit.* p. 83.

18. Steve Taravelia, "Defining the Hospital's Role: New CEO Expands Mission Beyond Healthcare," *Modern Healthcare*, December 8, 1989, p. 54.

19. Sally Berger, "Hospital Strengthens Ties to Doctors with Joint Venture," *Modern Healthcare*, January 29, 1988, p. 39.

20. Greene, *op. cit.*, p. 30.

21. Lawrence J. Nelson, H. Westley Clark, Robert L. Goldman, & Jean E. Schore, "Taking the Train to a World of Strangers: Health Care Marketing and Ethics," *Hastings Center Report*, September/October, 1989, p. 36 ff.

22. Sandy Lutz, "Planting the Seeds of Growth: He Turned One Hospital into a Rural Network," *Modern Healthcare*, May 12, 1989, p. 48.

23. *Ibid.*

24. *Ibid.*

Chapter 3

Applying Managed Service Restructuring

SENIOR MANAGEMENT INVOLVEMENT

It is not sufficient for senior management to give lip service to the restructuring or development of an organization's services. There must be commitment, accountability, and responsibility.

Commitment by the CEO and COO (Chief Operating Officer) is essential since resources are always scarce and developing or troubled projects cannot withstand financial or human resource cuts. Accountability, at a senior level, is critical since a program without a champion will be killed off rapidly. It is too easy to shrug off a service's outcome with a statement that senior management had nothing to do with it. In addition, there must be a senior person who has responsibility to make changes and fight for a service.

As Johnson and Boss state, "Patients faced with large health care bills justifiably expect high quality in return, in terms of up-to-date medical technology and attentive personal care. . . . Meanwhile continuity of care is complicated by shorter stays and increased specialization, plus the high use of out-patient and home care."[1] Thus, managers at all levels are under extreme stress to cut unnecessary services while retaining services essential to the maintenance of quality.

Reduced reimbursement is in conflict with the constant need to upgrade technology.[2] The hot seat is at the senior management level where it belongs since these people are expected to have an overview of organizational needs.

Furthermore, a second factor, excessive management turnover, impedes critical program analyses. One article cites several success factors in planning for management change. One of them is acceptance of responsibility and commitment to the process by senior management.[3] In addition, too much planning is sometimes based on the perceived need to build a record that will stand up under legal scrutiny instead of being of a practical nature.

These three negative factors usually combine to repress an MSR approach. For example, a 250-bed acute care hospital, was losing over $10 million per year when a new CEO took over.[4] Of course the first step was to attempt to cut every possible cost without affecting quality or alienating the medical staff.

Nursing FTE's were cut to a minimal level so that there was little time for nurses and physicians to communicate. In addition, ward clerks were eliminated. This forced registered nurses to take on the clerks' duties on top of their own. Because of these actions, morale sharply declined.

The new CEO's task was made even harder because the medical staff was divided into those whose centers of excellence had been supported by the previous administration and those who had not received support. The two centers, a sports medicine program and a cardiac surgery clinic, no longer had support from either the medical staff or the administrative team. Since these two centers had been inaugurated by the former CEO, who was now out of favor, they too lost support and lacked attention from the new team.

Since senior management was not familiar with the programs, effective restructuring was delayed until they got up to speed. By then, the CEO realized that these centers were of great potential value. However, they had no champion on the senior management team, they had not been marketed properly, their financial support from the hospital was excessive, and the physicians benefiting most were the least cooperative.

One fortunate factor was that the new CEO had been affiliated with the medical center the previous year. There were still good relations with many employees, administrators, and medical staff members.

The CEO ordered a complete analysis, similar to an MSR analysis, to be accomplished within three months. While those involved missed this deadline by a month, the analysis was thorough and gave the new CEO a sound basis for decision making.

The two centers were restructured. The hospital assisted in reframing the boards and administrations and their subsidies were cut. The centers were placed on a management by objective plan that required them to manage themselves more effectively.

Both centers, under these plans, were required to develop realistic objectives in the areas of procedures performed, new patients acquired, development of new referral sources, and the cutting of overhead. Instead of across-the-board cuts, the executive directors were mandated to present downsizing plans that reduced fat without cutting into the meat of the operations.

The centers' physicians were asked to eliminate travel to conventions that did not bring in new business. An international symposium, sponsored by one of the centers, was placed on a profitable basis by cutting frills such as glossy brochures.

Qualified marketing representatives were permitted to have a say in how the centers were to be promoted. For example, an advertising campaign that was avant guard in nature and very costly was killed and a more effective approach was used. The key to the success of the promotional approaches was that all four promotional methods, advertising, public relations, sales promotion, and personal selling, were controlled by the marketing representatives with approval by the administrators.

Thus, programs were coordinated and efforts were integrated into each program. After two years, one center is profitable while the other is breaking even despite an additional problem that arose when referrals were withheld by several key doctors.

As Andrew Grove says, "A manager must add value to the work of his or her employees. . . . [The] manager should cause his worker to become more productive, more efficient and capable of generating progressively high quality work."[5] He does that in many ways including sharing his superior technical knowledge, training employees, setting clear objectives, and creating an atmosphere in which employees are encouraged to make a contribution.[6]

SENIOR MANAGEMENT RESPONSIBILITY AND ACCOUNTABILITY

Senior management links the Board and the community to the administrative and medical staffs by being accountable for the organization's directions and communicating the mission to all.

However, one group outside managerial control is of singular importance to your hospital–the medical staff. Physicians interact with the hospital through a professional bureaucracy wherein controls are enforced through such techniques as peer review.[7] Their work must be supervised by those competent to assess clinical outcomes. But their affiliation and managerial interaction with the institution should be based on their business acumen. Senior management is the appropriate place for monitoring the interaction of the medical staff and the other parts of the hospital.

MSR requires that managers should be capable of taking a comprehensive or global view of the organization so that senior managers work in concert with the medical staff and others to bring each plan to fruition. However, senior management must delegate such activities as planning to a department head.

One survey states that less than 50 percent of hospitals have a planning department.[8] MSR cannot be accomplished unless there is a planning team to conduct research and analysis and develop planning documents for the review of senior management and other concerned parties.

MIDDLE MANAGEMENT'S ROLE

The reality of most organizations, especially those with extremely limited resources such as the typical health care institutional provider, is that senior management must trust and rely on middle managers. Often these managers treat their departments as petty kingdoms, leading to impediments in management communications and exacerbation of problems rather than the resolution of them.

APPROACHES TO IMPROVE QUALITY AND MSR

In practice, Quality Service (QS) initiatives provided by health care organizations must respond to the external customers' needs and promote internal employee participation in the process of creating positive customer experience.[9] It is difficult, if not impossible, to provide excellent service without having this collective organizational commitment or without providing the training and the resources necessary to support it.

QS improvement and enhancement is an ongoing process that demands constant renewal. Oftentimes, it can be overwhelming for an organization to even begin to implement a QS program. QS will also ensure that small inefficiencies and concerns do not advance into big problems in the future.

QS improvement is not intended as a program unto itself. Instead, it is a process that helps organizations manage their operations and customer relations in a supportive environment and a proactive, participatory "organizational culture." If Quality of Service efforts are successfully applied, they will help any organization become more proactive and avoid the types of problems the MSR approach is often called upon to reverse.

EMPLOYEE CONCERNS AND COOPERATION

An institution's employees are as critical to its success as any other constituency. Recently a major ambulatory care organization found this to be true. This association found that it offered technically high quality services. However, its employees did not interact well with each other or with a wide variety of customers including hospitals, physicians, community members, and volunteers.

A practical way for this organization to implement a QS program was to identify doable steps within a given time frame and to break down the work into manageable tasks. Action steps that were included in the first phase of the Quality Service Program (QSP) in the first 30-60 days included:

- Review specific customer recommendations developed through focus groups and presented to management in a report and address those that can be implemented immediately. These were not Band-Aids, but were simple solutions to problems that could create an immediate increase in customer satisfaction, employee morale, and operational efficiency. Once actions were selected, these were communicated to all employees through a series of "FYI" (informational) presentations, which included sharing the key findings of this survey research in the form of an oral presentation.
- The QSP concept was introduced and explained to the organization's management team in a one-day seminar featuring an outside expert.
- An implementation plan was developed which included budget and mandatory training policy guidelines for providing core management skills training in leadership, motivating employees, team-building, communications and listening, how to run meetings and projects, and other topics for all managers, officers, supervisors, and head nurses.

• A "Good Ideas From Good People" employee suggestion program was rapidly developed and implemented.

In Phase II, consisting of 60 days to six months, a Quality of Service Strategic Business Plan was developed by the Quality Service Steering Committee members. This was begun at a strategic retreat. This enabled the management team to include necessary budgetary resources within the next budget year that will be required to implement the strategies and tactics outlined in the QS Business Plan.

The long-term activity of the Quality Service Plan is driven by the strategies, tactics, and action steps that are identified by the QSP described above. Since measurable evaluation tools will be included, however, the plan and the activity must be reviewed at regular intervals and updated. This must be an ongoing process.

Managers need to develop systems in which divisional heads have a high level of autonomy, meetings are kept informal, there is a separation between strategic and operational processes, and roles and responsibilities are clarified.[10] When these principles are not followed, the MSR approach is difficult to apply.

Managers must be able to administer their department with as much of an operational free hand as possible in order for them to have confidence in their own decisions. While structured meetings are useful when large groups must rapidly process numerous agenda items, small informal meetings build trust and permit managers to share concepts without being placed in a negative position.

When roles and responsibilities are not clarified and strategic and operational processes are combined, the level of ambiguity is too high to permit unbiased analysis. Managers become fearful that a reduction in resources allocated to a program will decrease their status.

One author (Goldman) worked with a large ambulatory care organization, with over 300 employees and several delivery sites, that had not changed management or management styles for over 20 years. The original CEO retained an office at the organization's headquarters and often was asked for input on managerial and operational questions.

This organizational founder was considered to be a benevolent despot who had made all major decisions down to the level of the first line supervisors. While this former CEO had retired over five years prior to the latest management intervention, changes in policies and procedures were difficult to make. "We've always done it this way," was the standard response.

Interdepartmental communication was almost non-existent. Supervisors and managers expected to have decisions made at the highest level and were fearful that they would be criticized if they did take control.

An MSR analysis showed that resources were being wasted and most employees had little input into decisions. Programs were developed without regard to resources available or potential community need because one or more physicians asked for them.

The analysis found that department supervisors, whose departments were located near one another, rarely discussed joint problems. Front line employees, most familiar with operational bottlenecks, were seldom consulted. In most cases, supervisors took a passive role when problems or opportunities arose.

The person requesting the MSR analysis was the director of marketing. She convinced the COO and CFO to look at three aspects–operations, marketing, and finance–within one framework. This reduced developing conflicting goals and encouraged synergy.

For example, the marketing department previously had no say in the development of new services. As noted above, when a physician asked for a costly service, it was usually developed with no regard to community needs. Under the new methodology, marketing was asked for a needs analysis.

Part of the new approach taken was to develop an organization-wide effort to improve communications. An internal marketing campaign was designed and implemented over a two-year period. Managers and supervisors from all units were brought together to develop the plan. Focus groups were held to obtain input from employees, managers, and customers. The results were published and discussed.

Changes were divided into those that could be accomplished within 90 days and those that would require a longer period of time. Each service was evaluated by those directly involved and recommendations developed were reviewed by those who would have to implement them.

The most serious problem, the lack of interdepartmental communication, was addressed first. Supervisors were given time to meet informally with their counterparts in other departments. Each service line manager briefed middle managers on their programs and numerous cost-cutting recommendations resulted. This provider saw improvements in service quality and customer relations even as the process continued.

In effect the organization had entered into a continuing "Open Forum" designed to encourage nonthreatening service analysis.[11] The MSR approach is not completed on a given date or when a report has been presented. Middle management has an obligation to continuously apply the MSR approach to all services offered in order to keep pace with changes in the environment and the availability of resources.

WHEN AND HOW TO USE OUTSIDE CONSULTANTS

Outside consultants should be used when they have specific skills to offer that are not available within the organization and not for the purpose of enhancing the credibility or status of the institution. If the consultants offer a fresh view or extensive experience in a specialized field they can be of great value.

Managers should check credentials thoroughly. A firm should

not be hired simply because a consulting firm has a national reputation. Often, local consultants are knowledgeable, competent, and far less expensive.

Two problems are common with consultants. First, the senior consultant who sells the engagement may have little or nothing to do with the client. Second, the consultants working with the client may have little or no experience in the specific area under investigation.

The person responsible for coordination with the consultant should have the consultant make clear the roles and responsibilities of all members of the consulting firm. Hadelman states, "All too often, a senior partner will make the pitch but then delegate the assignment to a junior staff member who learns the business at the client's expense. Clients may not realize what's happening until a crisis develops and the junior staff member's lack of experience becomes all too evident."[12]

Marketing consultants are often the worst offenders. One should remember that many such consultants came out of government-based certificate-of-need planning or public relations and have little or no experience in market-based strategic planning or analysis. While these consultants can follow the MSR approach step-by-step, they lack the insight to distinguish fine points that may be critical to success.

A consultant is a change agent whose activities will disturb the organization. However, such a consultant can act as a facilitator for change when those within the organization cannot. You should always choose "One-Handed" consultants. That is, those who are not always saying, " . . . but on the other hand." Work with consultants who are willing to make a recommendation and stand behind it.[13]

Often, following a national consulting firm is overly profitable to the new consultant and frustrating and costly to the client. One such national firm developed a negative report for a specialized ambulatory care center that was to be supported by a regional hospital. The national firm misunderstood the nature of tertiary services and stated that demand was limited to the local area.

Even though there was an unmet need for this service regionally, the project was stalled for five years. A local consultant attempted to develop a realistic approach but was stymied by the reputation of the national consultant and the lack of knowledge on the part of the key physician.

A third consultant (Goldman) was asked to attempt to develop a plan that would get the project off and running. The MSR approach was successfully implemented. In this case, it was demonstrated that the center would not rely on a local patient base because the center would attract patients from a wide geographic area. A second concern was that specialists would object to the hospital's support of the center because it would draw business from them.

The first step was to develop a demographic analysis of the region. The total number of patients with needs available only through the center was determined by using secondary data and conducting interviews with experts in the field.

Next, the specific services to be offered were described and a determination was made of what competition existed. It was found that the local specialists would not consider the center to be their competitor because of the narrow scope of the services. Instead, most indicated that they would support the center since they saw that the need being filled was, in truth, unmet.

There were two competitors on a national basis. However, they were widely spaced and provided mutual support. Both these centers were affiliated with the same hospital network with which the new center would be affiliated. This offered a synergy that had not been seen by the original consultants. Regional competitors did not offer a complete package of services and were not considered to be a major threat.

The marketing element included a description of all services, how they would be priced, proposed service sites, and a basic promotional plan. Since the plan involved nonprofit hospital funding for a for-profit center, legal issues such as inurement were analyzed.

The financial analysis demonstrated that the center would break even during its second year of operation, not during the fifth year as previously thought because of the regional scope of the project. The original consultants had missed this point.

Within five months the hospital agreed to fund the center in the amount of $3 million. The center is moving according to plan. However, the progress is slower than expected due to internal delays.

ELIMINATING OPERATIONAL BIAS

Operational bias has two components. First, a reluctance to change despite new environmental imperatives. Second, an over-emphasis on technical quality at the expense of customer relations.

The excessive cost of health care can be partly attributed to operational bias. A recent poll found that only 3 percent of the population were dissatisfied with the quality of health care. However 24 percent rated the health care system as poor.[14]

Another study found that only 13 percent of corporate executives believed that they would be able to bring health care costs under control within two years.[15] Operational bias contributes to the problem when providers feel that they must have the latest diagnostic tool or they will lose out to the competitor. Often we see a new methodology such as CT scanning or magnetic resonance imaging follow a costly pattern.

When the new gadget hits the market in its most costly and inefficient form, competing hospitals will raid important programs to acquire the new toy. Once they have it in place, they often find that utilization is low because there are too many units in the market and physicians are unfamiliar with its capabilities.

To surmount this problem a costly promotional campaign tries to drum up business. Often, the result is that the campaign is successful in the sense that the new modality becomes popular. However, little thought is given to the use of previous, less costly techniques when their use would be appropriate.

To overcome operational bias the management team can identify channels of information relevant to the organization, then screen the information that fits its needs. In order to avoid the exclusion of external points of view, there should be some person or department responsible for the acquisition of competitive intelligence and a community advisory board that can represent the community's needs and feelings.

COMMUNITY INVOLVEMENT

Community involvement is more than community relations. The objective is to co-opt the community by listening to community representatives and offering alternatives for their review. Often the community's understanding of a health care organization's mission needs to be revitalized. "Evidence suggests many people think hospitals are in this business for the money." [16]

An institution should use multiple channels to obtain community input. A community advisory board is an excellent venue if the board is proactive and not merely a reactive group. Therefore, advisory and even governing boards must be well trained to accomplish their tasks. [17]

Interviews with community representatives and leaders are extremely valuable as are broader based surveys to determine attitudes and awareness of issues and programs. Active membership in the local chamber of commerce is also useful.

When a crisis hits, the community will play a major role in selecting the future track. Often, it will not be possible to develop a plan that meets the needs of all groups.

Your goal will probably be acceptance rather than enthusiasm.

If you present your point of view and your options in a realistic manner, you will find that the level of trust will be high and your community will support you even if they are not happy with the moves you have to make.

The authors know a public health manager in charge of a medically indigent adult health care program that established strong credibility with providers by giving them current and accurate information on all issues. As state funds were cut back, he had a choice of tightening eligibility standards or cutting reimbursement.

He presented his options at meetings with recipients and providers and found that both groups wanted the other to shoulder the burden caused by the state's action. However, when he laid out realistic scenarios, the providers accepted reimbursement cuts. They were not happy, but they did accept the decision.

When considering eliminating a service, bring your community into the process as soon as possible. You may find that they may suggest options that you had not considered. Trust your customers.

MEDICAL STAFF PARTICIPATION

Like the community, the medical staff is important to the acceptance of new programs within your facility. Without medical staff support, no program can succeed. We have all seen cases in which the medical staff has fired senior executives because they could not win over the physicians to their point of view. While the medical staff is independent of the hospital, it controls a bureaucracy of its own.[18] Its members have significant impact on the administration with few controls on the part of the hospital's administrators.

The best method of keeping the medical staff in a positive frame of mind is to include representative members in the planning process. A genuine commitment to listen to their thoughts and respond to their needs will make the process much easier. However, if the participants are expected to approve plans that have already been finalized, the process will break down and support will be lost.

Another important factor to consider is the differences in compensation between administrators and physicians. Administrators are paid to attend meetings while doctors must take time from their practices causing them to lose immediate revenue as well as put in extra hours to make up for time spent in each meeting.

Unless this problem is overcome, you will find that physicians will tend to miss meetings and not take the time to be prepared when they do attend. While legal counsel needs to be consulted on the issue of inurement, it is often possible to compensate physicians for their planning activities.

Physicians also need to be brought up to speed on business skills such as how to read and interpret financial and marketing reports. A review of business skills will prove invaluable.

DEALING WITH COMPETITORS

While you must be careful not to enter into anti-competitive practices, you will still have to deal with your competitors in many situations. There will be times when your organization does not possess the capability to provide all the services your community or clients need. For example, several hospitals and physician groups may join together to form a provider network to service a large, multi-site employer.

You may also find that you or your competitor have a service that is located within the wrong institution. An obstetrics program may be failing in a community hospital where the population has aged but could do well in a regional hospital dedicated to serving women and children even when they are located in the same area.

Another interaction is the development of market intelligence about your competitors. Legitimate means such as reviewing government reports and statistics, following your competitors' public announcement, and gaming are valuable tools.

If you assign an internal team the task of developing competitors' marketing strategies, based on available data, you will find that you can predict, with a high degree of accuracy, what your competitors will do. Knowing the resources of a competitor will give you a fairly good idea about what their strategies will be.

Gaming can often be more accurate than complicated forecasting techniques. A related tactic is to find tomorrow's experts in assessing your market and testing their predictions against reality. Futurists, however, have a short useful life. Too often they become accepted experts. Then they play it safe, their predictions become conventional and their value is reduced.

THE JOINT VENTURE APPROACH

The hospital–physician joint venture has come under scrutiny because of anti-trust concerns.[19] However, concepts that are designed to be reasonable business ventures, instead of a tool to capture physician loyalty through disguised kickbacks, can succeed. There are three tests that each venture should pass to avoid anti-trust problems:

1. What is the competitive impact of the rearrangement on the market in which the venture operates?
2. What is the venture's competitive impact on other markets in which some or all of the ventures compete?
3. What is the impact on competition of any ancillary restrictions contained in a joint venture agreement?[20]

For small ventures, the degree of physician investment is critical in that specific formulae determine what is considered a violation of the Medicare Fraud and Abuse regulations.[21]

The joint venture form that appears to have the highest potential for success is the Integrated Delivery System (IDS) in which hospitals, physicians, and other providers form a business organization that has the capability of accepting managed care contracts from large, regional health plans and also directly contracting with employers. The IDS is discussed in Chapter 4.

REFERENCE NOTES

1. James A. Johnson & R. Wayne Boss, "Management Development and Change in a Demanding Health Care Environment," *Journal of Management Development*, Vol. 10, No. 4, 1991, p. 5.

2. *Ibid.*, p. 6.

3. S. Robert Hernandez, Cynthia Carter Haddock, William M. Behrendt & Walter F. Klein, Jr., "Management Development and Succession Planning: Lessons for Health Service Organizations," *Journal of Management Development*, Vol. 10., No. 4, 1991, p. 24.

4. Note: One of the authors, Robert Goldman, was directly involved in this situation.

5. Andrew S. Grove, *One-On-One with Andy Grove*, Penguin, New York, 1987, p. 38.

6. *Ibid.*

7. Daniel S. Fogel, "The Uniqueness of a Professionally Dominated Organization," *Healthcare Management Review*, Summer, 1989, p. 156.

8. "Less Than 50% of Hospitals Have Planning Departments," *Modern Healthcare*, May 7, 1990, p. 39.

9. Among numerous articles on TQM and CQI are the following: "CEO's Say Hospitals Must Learn from Each Other for TQM Success," *Hospitals*, June 20, 1992 pp. 42 ff.; Emily Friedman, "What Do Consumers Really Want?" *Healthcare Forum*, May/June 1986, pp. 19 ff.; and, "Buying Into Customer Service," *Training & Development*, September, 1991, pp. 11 ff.

10. Karen Lowson, "Changing Structures for Resource Management," *Public Finance and Accountancy*, Nov. 22, 1991, p. 15.

11. Charles McConnell, "Collaborative Management Development: Sharing a Wealth of Ideas and Experience," *Journal of Management Development*, Vol. 10, No. 4, 1991, pp. 12-13.

12. Jordan Hadelman, "Here's What to Ask When Hiring Search Firm," *Modern Healthcare*, September 23, 1991, p. 32.

13. Robert L. Goldman & Brenda K. Klopatick, "Developmental Steps in the Formation of a Professional Provider Group or Independent Practice Association," *Journal of Hospital Marketing*, Vol. 2 (1), 1987, p. 107.

14. Michael Schachner, "Health Care Quality Good, but System is Poor: Pool," *Business Insurance*, October 28, 1991, p. 2.

15. Jerry Geisel, "U.S. Executives Call for Health Care System Reform," *Business Insurance*, December 23, 1991, p. 42.

16. Arthur Sturm, "Move Now to Communicate Your Mission to the Public," *Modern Healthcare*, September 23, 1991, p. 21.

17. Carol Molinari, Laura Morlock, Jeffrey Alexander, & Alan Lyles, "Hospital Board Effectiveness: Relationships Between Board Training and Hospital Financial Viability," *Health Care Management Review*, Vol. 17, No. 3, Summer, 1992, p. 43.

18. Fogel, *op. cit.*, p. 16.

19. See the Tax Reform Act of 1986 and related laws and regulations.

20. P.E. Jose, "Antitrust and Joint Ventures," *Topics in Health Care Financing*, Fall, 1986, p. 59.

21. These regulations vary from one venture to another. An attorney should be consulted.

Chapter 4

Preventing Service Line Deterioration

ONGOING SITUATION ANALYSIS

Analyzing your strategic situation is essential for the successful operation of any health care facility. Even though your goals and objectives are reviewed and revised annually, the environment can change more rapidly than anticipated. This can cause obstacles to be placed in the way of achieving your objectives.

Of course, your operational plan will attempt to include all foreseeable changes. The key element in which potential changes would be included is the SWOT or situation analysis discussed in the market analysis section of Chapter 2.[1]

The experiences and analytical capabilities of the administrative team plays an essential part in implementing a successful plan. Managers should use brainstorming to arrive at all possible approaches and outcomes for each segment of the plan. Chow et al., have suggested an approach that they call "Fault Trees," to develop a strategic plan that anticipates problems which could affect the overall project directly or by affecting the subsystems and components of the project.[2]

They suggest that the typical situation analysis is too subjective. By using an analysis technique called prospective hindsight, this problem can be reduced.[3] Thus, the development of fault trees permits troubleshooting before the project begins or at the earliest stage possible. The authors explain their method by stating, "Constructing a fault tree generally begins with limbs. If the focus of a fault tree is threats or problems, building limbs would involve identifying major areas (or subsystems) where problems may cause the overall project (or system) to fail. Next comes branches, the major individual components whose failure could lead to subsystem failure. Finally, twigs are lists of specific components of a given subsystem to fail. Once constructed, a fault tree is a useful troubleshooting guide, providing not only an efficient way to eliminate different explanations and to guide data collection but also a structure for estimating the probability that the entire operation or specific subparts will fail. Conversely, a fault tree can provide a framework for identifying events or actions that would lead to success."[4] As the authors point out in their last comment, a fault tree may be used in a positive way. We suggest that the two methods be used in order to both avoid failure and ensure success.

Thus, in developing a new free-standing imaging center, you would look at positive areas such as the involvement of your medical staff and the demonstrated need for the new center as well as such negatives as Medicare Fraud and Abuse regulations and your competitors. Your analysis would be strengthened by the detail that the fault tree approach forces you to include.

NEW SERVICES: GAIN CONSENSUS PRIOR TO LAUNCH

It goes without saying that a thorough understanding of your institution's mission, clientele, and present and potential markets must be analyzed before starting a new service. Once research determines the utility of the proposed service, you must build consensus among administrators and participating staff to accept and promote the service. Consensus building requires more time than having management order that all participate in implementation. Consensus building usually requires plan modification and realignment of resources and participants. However, the time spent on consensus building will often be saved when you begin to implement the project and find that everyone is on board.

A note of caution is appropriate here. Consensus alone does not build successful programs. Finding the right market segment is essential. For example, developing a strategic business unit (SBU), or as MacStravic calls them, "Strategic Program Units," based on the desire to penetrate the geriatric market through the development of a seniors membership program may be accepted by all.[5] However, in this situation you must look at what your competitors are doing and also develop a program that meets the needs of the seniors.

Porter calls this "focus."[6] Focus, along with overall cost leadership and differentiation, is one of three generic strategies for outperforming competitors. It is defined as, " . . . a corporate concentration strategy that focuses on a particular buyer group."[7] Porter states that, "the focus strategy has two variants: *cost focus* and *differentiation focus*." He notes that the target segment may have buyers with unusual needs or that the production and delivery system may vary from what is needed in other segments.[8]

Porter concludes that a successful SBU must achieve one of these three generic business strategies. In attempting to increase quality managed care contracts, for example, many hospitals have failed because they used the wrong strategy. When using the overall cost leadership strategy, a hospital that attempts to "Buy the Business" with constant low bids may find itself losing money on all contracts.

Therefore, by switching to a focus strategy, the hospital will be able to differentiate between contracts. A Medicare risk contract will require different service and cost assumptions than a worker's compensation contract in an area with a predominance of light industry. By focusing on customer needs and wants instead of on the desire of your firm's managers, you will be able to acquire new business that will meet your revenue requirements.

THE DEVELOPMENT OF CENTERS OF EXCELLENCE

If an organization determines that it will offer a service in the premier setting in its region, it will usually make every attempt to keep that service current and will avoid deterioration of quality. One strategy that has become both popular and successful is that of developing centers of excellence.

An article in *Hospitals* discusses how the concept is successfully applied in hospitals around the country.[9] In one study, ". . . 57 percent of hospital CEOs reported that they had designated one or more services as a priority program. Approximately 44 percent reported that they had selected three or more programs for development."[10]

One article with an emphasis on nursing discusses the concept of the Magnet Hospital. The authors make the point that such hospitals maintain staffing levels even during shortages.[11]

Another article offers a methodology to increase hospital revenue through the use of such centers with a direct approach to potential patients.[12] The article cites various studies that review hospital selection for different services and the highest patient selection rates were in women's services.[13]

The article noted that centers of excellence and the hospitals that sponsor them may have greater approval ratings in the eyes of the public.[14] The authors cite studies that state that patients' attitudes toward a hospital may be enhanced by positive attitudes toward a particular center or group of centers of excellence.[15] Their point is that centers can help build image and that a positive image is essential for continued success.

This point of view, that centers of excellence are needed for hospitals to continue to prosper, is discussed by Jeff Goldsmith.[16] He makes three points:

- Hospitals are more than merely businesses.[17]
- He states that hospitals have a new mission to treat those with chronic problems.[18]
- Another point that Goldsmith makes is that doctors remain at the center of health care delivery and that hospitals will continue to find it essential to collaborate with doctors in taking care to the community.[19]

Coile also states that "Techno-niches" or centers of excellence are essential for continued success.[20] Coile discusses the concept of national networks in health care. While many of us have expected to see these as dominant forces, their potential still is to be met. (Coile states that 90 percent of hospitals will be affiliated within four years.)[21]

Barich and Kotler encourage organizations to track their images and take steps to achieve or maintain a positive image.[22] They state that each image factor is made up of a number of attributes among which are products (or services) offered. Characteristics such as the quality and reliability of a service are cited as directly affecting this image.

It is obvious that well-respected centers of excellence positively affect image and therefore revenues. Claus states that health care organizations are in an environment that is constantly changing.[23] To retain market share, hospital administrators must be innovative and dedicated to managing change. In addition, they must overcome traditional barriers to working with physicians.

Hospitals are developing numerous centers of excellence, notes an article in *Hospitals*.[24] The author makes the point that priorities must be set when developing new services and that resources should not be spread too thinly.

Sheldon S. King of Cedars-Sinai Medical Center of Los Angeles found it beneficial to cooperate with UCLA Medical Center to avoid unnecessary competition thereby serving the region more appropriately by focusing on services that the centers are best at providing.[25] King also stated that hospitals should go beyond health care and provide services to the community such as access to proper housing, adequate nutrition, and counseling after discharge from the hospital. Of course, many hospitals do provide these services at this time. (We suggest that affiliations with voluntary health agencies such as the American Heart Association, the American Lung Association, or the Arthritis Foundation also may be beneficial. Consider the situation when a hospital patient is a member of an HMO. These agencies can provide important services and not deplete the capitation payment.)

John D. Hicks, CEO of North Mississippi Medical Center, restructured his hospital by developing a network of seven rural hospitals.[26] Previous to this effort he had merged two hospital-based ambulance services together in order to provide better service. In this situation, Hicks converted county-owned hospitals into a private, not-for-profit health care network.

In Lee County, hospital managers wanted the hospital to grow while the county officials were not interested in expansion. He bought the hospital's assets from the county for $25 million and restructured obsolete hospitals into a network that meets the needs of today's rural Mississippi residents.

Humana uses the centers of excellence concept as a corporate strategy. Humana Corporation began developing its Centers for Excellence program in 1982.[27] As of 1988, 17 of Humana's 25 hospitals had such centers. The centers are designed to increase admissions and prestige. Since a large patient base is required for a center, they are limited to large, metropolitan facilities. The centers also help enhance the physicians' practices.

Torrance (California) Memorial Medical Center divested itself of four of its major outpatient services to a for-profit joint venture with its medical staff. The new entity, Health Access Systems, averted competition from members of the medical staff, expanded market share, increased revenue and built a well-capitalized base for further ventures. By providing more than one service, the new corporation had a major competitive advantage.[28]

THE INTEGRATED DELIVERY SYSTEM

The rising trend of Integrated Delivery Systems (IDS), while offering an alternative means of physician-hospital cooperation, requires extensive planning and coordination between the two groups. Only an identifiable planning unit can do this. An IDS's corporate function is to operate a fully integrated health care delivery service, which includes entering into payor contracts, providing hospital and physician services, and collecting all revenue.[29]

The IDS format is an MSR response to changes in the environment. In one model, the Management Service Organization (MSO), integration is not complete, but managerial services are purchased by all players from the MSO. In the IDS model, each pre-existing organization is moved under one corporate umbrella either through outright purchase, an exchange of stock, or a donation to a nonprofit foundation with significant tax benefits.

An MSO or IDS restructures the ownership or management of its component parts in order to improve competitive position, recruit physicians, and lower overhead. The MSR approach dictates that these new organizations function in a manner that is consistent with the institutions' mission statement rather than be solely profit oriented.

An IDS usually requires more than one hospital, physicians organized into integrated groups or Independent Practice Associations (IPAs), and an information system that can integrate inpatient, out-patient, and ambulatory care in the areas of medical records, billing, and other related fields. Two forms of organization have proven successful: the foundation model and the management services organization (MSO) model. Usually, the move toward an IDS is initiated by a hospital or hospital system that approaches physicians to participate. Under the foundation model, ownership of hospitals and groups is transferred to a nonprofit foundation. The MSO model is less integrated. Ownership need not be transferred, but management is delegated to the MSO.

Since an IDS redefines its market from local to regional, antitrust issues appear to be less important, but still need to be settled. In effect, the IDS is a major step in industrializing health care delivery. The IDS provides economies of scale, the ability to offer care in customer oriented settings, and a reduction of administrative work for physicians. If the IDS fulfills its potential, patients will find doctors more accessible, employers will see cost reductions and there will be even less need for government regulation of providers.

DEVELOPING THE OPERATIONAL PLAN

Once the decision to form a provider network has been made, the following actions should be taken within a short time.

Form a steering committee consisting of senior members of all the parties involved in the project. This team should include a person with primary responsibility for managing the project and evaluating the plan.

Next, several issues need to be addressed, such as:

- Plan administration
- Provider relations
- Special, nonpanel providers
- Reporting/coordination
- The breadth of services to be offered
- Use of physician extenders
- Patient education

* Geography–rural vs. urban coverage
* Billing and collections
* Joint purchasing
* Controlling costs of special services such as mental health and rehabilitation
* Inclusion of nontraditional organizations such as voluntary health agencies

An *ad hoc* committee of physicians to develop and lead the provider panel should also be formed. One important task of this committee is to formulate provider selection criteria. The following criteria will help achieve qualitative and economic results without causing enmity within the medical community:

* Admitting privileges at a participating hospital
* Malpractice coverage as set by the provider panel
* Willingness to accept restrictions based on QA/UR protocol
* No major difficulties with the state licensing board
* Board eligibility or certification
* Willingness to accept discounted fees and/or capitation
* Willingness to pay dues and accept other obligations of membership such as committee participation
* Willingness to accept patients from all purchasers with whom the group contracts
* Willingness and ability to provide "frugal" care

Frugal care is distinguished by the attempt to cut nonessentials rather than across-the-board cuts that often force reductions in service quality.

At this time, the provider panel is ready to develop its utilization management protocol. The document establishes procedures to review credentials, analyze utilization, and assure quality.

They should also determine provider panel organization legal structure. Each type of legal entity has its good points. The options to be reviewed are: association, partnership, or corporation. The *ad hoc* committee should also develop a proposed committee structure that encourages participation by all members and assures that all important areas are covered. Committees must have real utility and not exist merely for an organizational chart. Here are some that appear useful:

- Executive Committee
- Credentials, QA/UR Committee
- Contract Negotiation Committee
- By-Laws Committee
- Finance Committee

At this time, a formal vote may be taken to elect a Board of Directors and approve the organization's structure. The group is now ready to complete its administrative set-up by hiring personnel and opening its office.

If the members have little experience with managed care, a series of orientation sessions will be useful. Topics might include:

- Elements of managed care
- Changes in employee/provider relations
- How to benefit from managed care and capitation in particular
- How the group will operate

The initial reimbursement mechanism should be set prior to accepting the first contract. Usually, a withhold is included in order to insure financial viability of the group. Other policies and procedures should be developed at this time as needed.

Once the operating system and staff are in place and tested, the group is ready to accept contracts and prepare for capitation. Perhaps the most important element is the true integration of the hospitals with the provider panel in the areas of financial controls, reporting, and incentives and management.

Success depends on all entities moving in the same direction. The key to this success is that the incentive for all providers be of the same type. If the contract is based on capitation, the hospital, primary care physicians (PCPs), and specialists all need to be rewarded in the same manner. A point of conflict will be between the PCPs and the specialists concerning who will provide a particular service. When both groups are capitated, each will want the other to provide care and carry the expense. IDS/MSO management will need to help develop protocols to solve this problem.

ENCOURAGE INNOVATION AT ALL LEVELS

To encourage innovation at all levels, you must go beyond incentives and open-door policies. As part of the MSR approach, you need to use every available tool to bring new ideas forward. Perhaps the easiest of these is the production and dissemination of your strategic plan in as simple and understandable a format as possible.

KEEP YOUR STRATEGIC PLAN SHORT AND SIMPLE

Your plan should be no longer than 25 to 35 pages. Supporting materials can be of any length but need to be kept out of the main body of the plan. You should expect to update the plan when changes occur instead of at a given time during the year.

A story the authors heard illustrates the point. We must go back to the 1950s and the Cleaver household: Ward, June, Wally, the Beaver, and of course Eddie Haskell.

June must have some kind of operation and will be in the hospital for three weeks. The boys can't take care of themselves. (Of course, this is the 1950s.) Hazel is hired away from her television show to manage the household. She does a perfect job including cooking their favorite dishes every evening for dinner. When June returns she asks Hazel how she did it. Hazel's reply is, "Simple, I just looked for the greasy pages in the cookbooks."

That is the kind of strategic plan that keeps organizations current. Plans that are greasy, dog-eared, and discussed by people at all levels of the organization are most effective. Avoid plans with dust on them. They never leave the shelf from year to year.

As seen in successful MSR approaches, periodic meetings with representatives of each element of your organization's community will also solicit new ideas. But this works only when the participants are made to feel that they have real input and are not just being appeased with presentations on decisions that have already been made.

QUALITY COMES IN TWO PARTS

Much has been said about customer service and quality improvement. Please note that there are two significant elements to any program and both must be of high quality if the appellation Total Quality Management is to be used.

Operational Quality: the services provided must be of high quality and offered with all essential support services in place. You may have a state-of-the-art CT scanner, however if your appointment program or billing is below par, you will find it difficult to provide quality service. To achieve operational quality in a service industry such as health care, your operational system must match your delivery system.

Health care can be divided into intermittent and continuous systems.[30] Within a hospital, the hotel function must operate continuously at a high level of service. However, the emergency department is subject to fits and starts and still must be ready to meet customer needs rapidly.

Intermittent systems are inefficient and subject to wide variances in quality control. If we can modify the operating system of our organization toward a continuous type system, we may be able to develop operating leverage. This is the impact a given change makes on the profitability and efficiency of the organization.[31] For example, the emergency department with high variable costs and intermittent activity may be marketed differently.

The department may be reframed to a standby level with minimal staffing. The nursing staff would be given the primary job of stabilizing patients for transport with physicians on-call. While admission would decline, net revenue might increase because of decreased expenses. One hospital system saw that its approach of using a small rural hospital for acute inpatient care was failing. Acute admissions average one per month while long-term care admissions were in the 20 per month range. Staffing was based on the emergency department bringing in four acute admissions per month. The physicians within this rural area did not want to use the hospital in the manner that the network had planned. After extensive research and analysis the process was changed to accommodate community desires and transport was emphasized.

Another strategy is to use the centers of excellence concept to expand the emergency department and attract regional business. Thus, the department can develop a continuous system in regard to staffing and related resources.

During the 1970s, the concept of regional trauma centers was developed in California. At one time there were 51 of these centers throughout the state. Many succeeded because of a high need for trauma response in their geographic areas. Others were terminated when their need was not established. Those still operating are extremely busy and operate under a continuous type of management system.

Quality Customer Service: untrained or uncaring employees who do not interact with your publics in a customer-oriented way are deadly to providing quality service. Recently a physician friend complained that the medical staff secretary was inefficient and was hurting a new physician education program. The doctor was concerned that perhaps this employee was reflecting the administration's attitude toward the new program. It turned out that the employee was overworked and poorly trained. However, this employee's inability to accommodate the doctor could have caused resentment with a potential for decreased admissions.

The cliché "there are no small parts, only small actors," should be applied in all of our organizations because each employee is important to our customers.

A NOTE OF CAUTION ABOUT TQM

TQM or Total Quality Management has at least one basic flaw. It is that managers and other employees must work at their optimal level of efficiency and competence. This is an unrealistic goal. Even the best people can have bad days. There are four problems that may arise to foil the TQM approach:

1. The decision maker or service provider did not receive necessary information.
2. The key person who interacts with customers is not motivated.
3. Even when the employee is informed and well motivated, situations change.
4. Employees have no guidance for decision making in unusual situations.

A patient is told to provide a blood specimen at the local hospital. The home health staff person informs the lab supervisor about the specifics of the situation. When the patient arrives at the appointed time, there is no record for the lab person on duty to refer to. The patient is delayed while a decision is guessed at. Finally, the blood is drawn but there is no follow-up and the home health agency must retrace every step to find the specimen.

This frustrating situation is very common. No one intended for it to happen, but the employee on duty did not have the latest information and had no guiding principle for such a situation.

One approach would be to accept reality and acknowledge that any or all of these four problems will usually occur. Murphy's Law cannot be broken. However, you can anticipate the situation.

For each critical factor for success, you should develop a guiding principle. You determine what is the lowest common denominator (LCD) in each situation and develop an approach that defaults to a customer-oriented result. You use a fail-safe approach.

An example of an LCD/Fail-Safe principle would apply in the lab situation. The employees on duty would be empowered to collect specimens or provide other customer service within their scope of employment. When in doubt, the employee would be able to take action. In this case, the specimen would be drawn and a record initiated even though there was no order or physician authorization on record.

Employees would help develop the guiding principles for the critical factors for success that impact their department or unit. Each principle would deal with a high level of ambiguity. In the event that the principle could not be implemented, a call to a supervisor would always be appropriate. There would never be a time when an employee would tell a customer that no one was available to help.

This LCD/Fail-Safe approach is designed to improve quality where it counts most: when the customer is in a hurry or has a high level of anxiety. It is not designed to circumvent standing policies, but gives employees at all levels the ability to respond during an emergency. An additional value of this approach is that employees have another motivator in the area of customer service.

Maintaining a high level of customer service is one of the best methods of retaining current clients and attracting new ones.

Two concepts currently in favor, Total Quality Management and Continuous Quality Improvement (CQI) dominate recent thought. This chapter builds on these concepts and the basic principles of marketing to simplify the implementation process. For want of better terms, the authors have adopted "LCD" (Lowest Common Denominator) and "Fail-Safe" to describe this approach. LCD encourages simplification so that the newest and least-trained employee will be able to work within the system. A Fail-Safe system is designed to be "Customer Friendly" even when an error takes place.

CUSTOMER SERVICE

Customer Service Is Key to Marketing Your Organization

Managed care will force you into an even more competitive environment than you have had to deal with so far. Potential members (customers) will have a choice between the plans you participate in and others based on competitive facilities. You will have a two-step sales process. First, you will have to sell the managed care organization, then you will need to sell the employer. To do so, you will have to meet the needs of the ultimate consumer: your patient/member/customer. Your marketing efforts will emphasize the utility of your organization. That is, you provide your customers with what they want, when they want it, in the form they want, and with the ability to use it to their purposes.

It is no longer possible to follow the ancient rule, "Build a better mouse trap and the world will beat a path to your door." This has been the traditional marketing approach within health care. Now, you must adopt the Marketing Concept. You are required to build products and develop services that are profitable and also fit the needs of your customers as closely as possible. For example, a community hospital with outpatient services limited to same-day surgery and basic emergency services may have to develop an industrial medicine/occupational health program to meet the needs of its employer base. Another example would be the extension of clinic hours or the development of an off-campus site designed to meet member needs.

Customer Service as Related to Marketing Research

Marketing research is the basis for customer service. By conducting valid research you will be able to determine what services (and goods) your customers want and need. You will be able to design packaging, such as a standard managed care service contract, that is attractive.

Marketing research will help you outsell your competitors because you will be able to better meet customer needs than ever before. It will also guide you in developing features to include in your product or service. You might find it easy and cost effective, for example, to offer a featured service such as an extra service obstetrical package that will attract customers/members. Based on the Marketing Concept, you will develop services that customers want rather than those your providers choose to offer.

Customer Service as Related to New Service Development

When developing new services (or products), you must design them to meet customer needs. You must also train your employees to offer them in ways that best satisfy your customers. You will have to build a customer service approach into new services along with their physical features such as clinic hours.

Your plan booklet or hospital literature must be easy to read with instructions that any customer can follow. If you offer a customer service telephone number, it must be easy for your customers to reach and the people answering the calls must be well trained in technical matters as well as in customer relations. If a customer finds the number is busy or the people answering the phone are abrupt in the way they answer questions, your customer may change plans during the next open enrollment period.

Customer Service as Related to TQM and CQI

TQM is a method designed to offer your customers goods and services of the highest quality. CQI is designed to reduce errors to a level of insignificance. Both techniques require that *every person within your organization perform his or her work without error*. As you well know, and as you will see in these materials, this type of effort is hard to achieve and even harder to sustain. The LCD/Fail-Safe concept is designed to help you achieve the highest level of customer service with the minimum amount of training and supervision by offering you realistic concepts.

Customer Service in the Retail Selling Situation

Working directly with your customers in a retail situation is the most difficult customer service environment. Unlike business customers, your retail customers often are not sure what they want or how to obtain it. You must be prepared to guide them toward what they want. A new patient in your hospital is in your retail setting for the first time. You may sell pharmaceuticcals, eye glasses, durable medical equipment, or hearing assistive devices through a retail unit.

LCD/FAIL-SAFE: A NEW CUSTOMER SERVICE APPROACH

Why TQM/CQI Often Does Not Achieve Its Goal

TQM/CQI requires every member of an organization to understand what is needed and to fill needs without errors. While working to eliminate or reduce errors and continuously cutting error tolerances are excellent concepts, they are extremely difficult to achieve. There are three reasons for this:

1. Some people do not get the correct information.
2. Not all employees are motivated to take the correct action.
3. The situation has changed since the information was last updated.

The key concept to remember is that we are all human and that we do make mistakes. Once we take this into account, we can work to build a system that will always err on the side of good customer service; that is a system which is "Customer Friendly."

EMPLOYEES DO NOT ALWAYS HAVE THE CORRECT INFORMATION

Telephone numbers change as do the job assignments of your employees. Often, the jobs themselves change and new people join your organization. Frequently, these evolutionary changes go by unnoticed. But, since change is a natural part of doing business, the goal must be to develop a system that is easy for employees to use when they need to find new information.

There are two elements to such an information system:

a. a hierarchical data bank
b. an expert.

Developing a Hierarchical Data Bank

Most information resources provide you with the data that you want and need at the same level. That is, all the information is arrayed by subject with a few headings. You are expected to read the information sequentially until you find what you want. This text is written in that manner. While it is fine for presenting new information, it requires more time than necessary when a specific piece of information is needed.

A hierarchical data bank presents information based on different levels. For example, an emergency directory might have three levels of specificity. Level One might be a list of key telephone numbers for each type of emergency. Level Two might give you instructions concerning how to deal with each non-usual event if no one is available.

For example, if a customer returns merchandise without a sales receipt, you may be given two or three options for dealing with the situation and suggestions for making a selection of one of the options. Level Three would provide more details than Level Two. Level Three information would show you each step in dealing with each option of the customer merchandise return situation. Included would be a listing of the forms you would use and instructions about how you would complete them.

For each emergency situation you would always have two fallback options. One would be to give the customer what they ask for. The other is to call an expert.

Using an Expert

An expert might be a senior administrative person. Regardless of the time or day, such a person should always be available to help solve customer service problems. It is inexcusable to tell a customer that they cannot be served because there is no one with authority available to help them. There must always be a person with authority available to solve customer service problems.

For example, a person is experiencing minor pain but there is no medication order. You must find a way to relieve that pain within your organization's procedures. You may have to call a stand-by or on-call physician if the attending doctor is not available. Unless the doctor refuses to authorize or prescribe medication, you may not leave the patient without pain control.

If your business is open at all hours and on every day, you must have a "Duty Manager" assigned to respond during those times when there are no managers working on-site. A Duty Manager knows the technical side of your business. More important, she or he has a thorough understanding of customer service and how to meet customer needs. The Duty Manager believes in and abides by the principle that the customer always comes first. The first principle of customer service is that the customer is always right.

EMPLOYEES ARE NOT ALWAYS MOTIVATED TO TAKE THE CORRECT ACTION

Even the best employee has an off day. Perhaps personal problems have high priority or there are too many customers in the clinic at the same time and there is not a method to prioritize them. When such a situation occurs, the customer does not receive the service he or she deserves. The result can be unhappy customers.

Managers at all levels need to observe their employees to attempt to maintain customer satisfaction. This is accomplished by spending as much time in the customer service areas as possible. While office time is essential to moving your organization forward, the time spent there does not solve customer service problems.

Walking the floors helps supervisors identify trouble spots before they cost the organization money. Preventive action is always preferable to correcting mistakes. In addition, there is a phrase that works wonders, "I am sorry, we made a mistake." This phrase acknowledges that we are all human and that you are willing to help your customers obtain what they need and want. Of course, correct follow-up action must be taken once the phrase has been stated.

The authors offer two situations that illustrate the point. A patient had successful surgery but experienced pain a few months later. An X ray showed that a foreign object had been left in the surgical wound. The doctor agreed to remove it, but wanted to bill the patient's insurance company for the procedure. The patient objected and states that the surgeon should bear the cost.

The other incident occurred when a patient experienced a severely broken femur resulting in a shortening of the leg. While the physician saved the patient's use of the limb, he did not inform him of a treatment, considered aggressive by the doctor, that could have avoided the length reduction. The patient feels that the doctor should have given him the information. The doctor was reluctant to admit his error nor did he apologize for withholding the information.

In both cases, the physicians should have apologized for their actions. In all likelihood, their competence would have been held in higher regard if they had done so. In the first case, a malpractice suit would have been avoided.

Consider the effect on your own people. To admit that you make mistakes informs them that you understand their situation. It also reduces the likelihood that they will find it necessary to cover up their errors.

THE SITUATION HAS CHANGED

Thriving organizations are in a state of flux. Procedures that were acceptable yesterday can cause problems today. The employee who is not aware that a change has taken place will not provide optimal customer service. To overcome this problem, we first assume that the problem will take place. Our employee and customer communication process is designed to be easy to understand.

We will also build in a redundancy factor so that everyone has multiple opportunities to get the new information. In addition, there will always be a Duty Manager available to help the employee or customer obtain the latest information.

Defining the LCD/Fail-Safe Concept

LCD stands for an idea that you will remember from your earliest mathematics classes. You learned that when you had several different fractions such as fifths and thirds that you had to find one fraction that was the lowest common denominator or LCD. If you were to add dissimilar fractions such as 2/3 and 3/5 you could convert them to 10/15 and 9/15. The LCD method permits you to work with the lowest common denominator in an organization: the newest, least trained–least motivated employee.

Fail-Safe is borrowed from a product design concept. For example, when designing pneumatic or air brakes for a truck, the system is fashioned so that if the air pressure falls below a given level the brakes will be applied. Thus, when the braking system fails, the probabiliy of harm to the truck is minimized. The system takes into account the knowledge that parts wear out and/or that maintenance may be faulty.

In a Fail-Safe customer service system the customer benefits even when the system is not working correctly. If a customer, for example, believes that her or his clinic room is unacceptable and, there is no way to correct the situation, the customer will be switched to a new room. If no better room is available, other services can be offered to compensate the customer, such as a reduced rate or elimination of copayments.

Why LCD/Fail-Safe Works

LCD/Fail-Safe works because it is understood that mistakes occur and it prevents the customer from suffering the consequences of those mistakes. Each customer is a valuable resource and is treated as such. Other TQM/CQI approaches work to eliminate mistakes in production or assembly situations such as in the operating room. They assume that people and systems can become error free and are less applicable in service organizations. Of course, this is not the case.

LCD/Fail-Safe thrives on potential and actual mistakes by encouraging employees and even customers to take corrective action at the first sign of a problem. Remember, your employees are customers in every sense of the word. Not only do they use your services, they must believe in them to be able to dispense them effectively. Your employees know that your organization is not perfect. They must have confidence that the system is designed to correct errors and not cover them up.

One of the best examples in recent years is how McNeil Company responded to the Tylenol poisoning disaster. No one at the time could expect that someone would poison Tylenol capsules causing the death of several people. McNeil Company managers responded rapidly by recalling the product from the market and by keeping the public informed. Some marketing experts stated that the company would never regain market share. They were wrong. Within a year of reintroducing Tylenol to the market, its share was larger than before the disaster.

LCD/FAIL-SAFE OBJECTIVES AND LIMITATIONS

Cost Effectiveness

If the system is not cost-effective you will not continue to use it. Therefore, LCD/Fail-Safe must improve your profit by retaining current customers and helping you obtain new ones through word-of-mouth promotion. We estimate that it costs as much as 30 percent of the first sale to acquire a new customer because of the high promotion costs. Thus, repeat customers offer greater potential profits and lower marketing expenses. Repeat customers have accepted you as an organization that is worth doing business with. They may have even become your advocate when mistakes take place. Your current customers are also your most powerful and least expensive method of acquiring new customers. When you advertise, you are stating your own case in the best way that you can. However, since we are all exposed to many such messages, we do not believe all that is said.

When a friend tells you that a product or service is worth using, you will probably believe that person. If the product or service does not stand up to the new customer's expectations, he or she will probably complain to the person who referred them to it. Your old customer may then want to enter the process of obtaining good customer service for your new customer.

Easy to Use

Your LCD/Fail-Safe system should have very few rules to follow so that those trying to implement it will find the new system to be easy for all to understand. Such rules as "The customer is always right" and "The customer comes first" are easy to follow.

Still, you must guard against the tendency to develop exceptions to these rules. For example, you have a standard opening time and a rule that no one is to be let into the office early. One day you see customers waiting five minutes before the appointed time. Let them in. You can explain that you are still preparing for the commencement of business and invite them to read magazines until you have completed your tasks. Do not let customers wait outside and allow them the opportunity to develop complaints about your facility or to become disappointed.

Another basic rule is that when a mistake is made, give the customer more than she or he asked for. If you do, you will have that customer for life. For example, you mistakenly bill a customer for a service not rendered. When your customer is informed of this error, she or he is told that the billing will not only be corrected but also that, because of the inconvenience caused, the copayment will be waived. Make it better than right.

Legal and Ethical

The long-term benefits of LCD/Fail-Safe are partly dependent upon all actions being both legal and ethical. It is wrong to solve a particular customer service problem while creating another problem that can harm your business. For example, in order to placate an unhappy customer, you provide her or him with confidential information. The basic principle here is to avoid all situations that even border on the unethical or illegal.

Based on the Principle of Equity

This may be the hardest principle to apply because it demands that all customers be treated on an equal basis even when each situation is unique. If two customers are overbilled, after correcting the billing problem, you would not want to offer one customer a copayment waiver and the other a free appendix transplant.

Since each situation varies, a set of rough guidelines should be developed with the thought that the employee working with the customer has some degree of latitude when dealing with a specific situation. Each compensation situation should be monitored by the appropriate manager and discussed during periodic staff meetings so that all employees get a feel for what is equitable.

Common Sense Must Govern

If a customer finds her or his coffee to be cold, a fresh cup of coffee and, perhaps, a free dessert is reasonable. You would not expect to waive that person's copayment in this case. In effect, the old adage, "the punishment should fit the crime," applies. That is, the reward should fit the mistake and be neither too small nor too large.

Do not make enemies by accident. You may have to tell a customer that you cannot meet her or his needs. You should still try to find others who can, and let your customer know about them. Claiming ignorance concerning other suppliers will back-fire when the customer discovers that you have been less than honest.

BUILDING THE LCD/FAIL-SAFE SYSTEM

Developing Critical Factors for Success (CFS) through Quality Work Circles (QWC)

Each unit of your organization should work as a QWC by accepting responsibility for monitoring its own quality. When em-ployees have the opportunity to criticize their own work in a non-threatening environment they will develop ways to improve it.

Defining your own CFSs is the best way to ensure that they are valid. A department's employees know where there is room for improvement and usually how to make a positive change. How-ever, there are times when your organization is unaware that it is not meeting customer standards. For example, when your cus-toms and business practices are different from those of your customers', you may be creating problems without being aware of the situation. When there is a potential for this to happen, you need to call for outside help such as consultants who are familiar with the wants and needs of these new customers. Do not rely on your own resources to dig out problems that you may not even know exist.

Going Below the Surface–Employee and Customer Empowerment

New customer service programs often have the result of sur-face success without true change. Your employees may be cheerful when dealing with customers but unless they also im-prove the way customer needs are met, this cheerfulness will not ring true. The nursing attendant who always cheerfully takes 20 minutes to respond to a request for service will cause your patients to complain about the quality of care. You must find out what the customer needs and provide it to them even if it forces you to increase staffing.

The Duty Manager

The Duty Manager is a CFS for your overall performance. This person must have a thorough knowledge of your business and also understand the principles of good customer service. There must always be a Duty Manager available who has the authority to solve customer service problems. The task of acting as Duty Manager should be an additional responsibility of all managers.

Do Not Place Blame

If employees feel that they will be blamed for an error when they must respond during an emergency, they will not accept responsibility to solve problems. Support their decisions once they are thoroughly trained to manage emergencies. Later each emergency or nonstandard situation can be analyzed to see how it could have been avoided and how the response could have been improved.

Learn from Actual Emergencies–Continuous Evaluation

As each emergency arises and is met, all managers and first-level employees should have the opportunity to see what went wrong and how the problem was solved. An open discussion at periodic meetings can help establish reasonable norms for future situations. These evaluation meetings can also develop new responses that have not been tried before. This is, in effect, the peer review process but extended throughout the organization.

Game Future Emergencies

When you start to analyze each element of your business for potential disasters, you will find that there is a limited number of options. While you cannot predict when a disaster will strike or who will be involved, you can develop reasonable responses to questions like the following:

a. What was the scope of the problem (department or organization wide)?
b. Who should respond?
c. What actions should be taken during the first few minutes? The first hour? The first days?
d. How will you respond to the media if they become involved?
e. Who will be in charge of follow-up actions?
f. Who will evaluate responses?

CONCLUSIONS

While the LCD/Fail-Safe concept is not infallible, it has the potential for improving customer service at a low cost with a minimum of problems. Remember the basic principles, apply them to the best of your ability, and you will see rapid improvement in customer satisfaction.

- Base your customer service on the Marketing Concept.
- Use marketing research to learn from your customers.
- The customer is always right.
- Make it better than right: give the customer more than she or he asked for.
- Keep your LCD/Fail-Safe system simple.
- Your responses to customer service problems must be legal and ethical.

- Your responses should be approximately equal in similar situations.
- Your employees at all levels are part of your customer service system.
- Go below the surface: a smiling employee who is incompetent does not help your organization.
- Learn from past problems and game potential predicaments.
- Do not make enemies by accident.

REFERENCE NOTES

1. Albert J. Sunseri & David B. Costeva, "Strategic Planning is Essential to Career Planning," *Healthcare Financial Management*, March, 1992, p. 100.

2. Chee W. Chow, Kamal Haddad & Barbara Miannino, "Planning Effectiveness May Grow On Fault Trees," *Healthcare Financial Management*, October, 1991, p. 36.

3. *Ibid.*

4. *Ibid.*

5. Scott Macstravic, "Market and Market Segment Portfolio Assessment For Hospitals," *Healthcare Management Review*, Summer, 1989, p. 25.

6. Michael E. Porter cited in: Thomas L. Wheelen & J. David Hunger, *Strategic Management and Business Development*, 3rd. Ed., Addison-Wesley, Reading, MA, 1989, pp. 220-221.

7. *Ibid.*

8. *Ibid.*

9. Therese Droste, "'Center of Excellence' name tag carries clout," *Hospitals*, July 20, 1989, p. 54.

10. *Ibid.*

11. Marlene Kramer & Claudia Schmalenberg, "Magnet Hospitals, Parts I & II, Institutions of Excellence," *JONA*, Vol. 18, No. 1, Jan. 1988, pp. 13 ff. and Vol. 18, No. 2, pp. 11 ff.

12. Scott M. Smith & Marta Clark, "Hospital Image and the Positioning of Service Centers: An Application in Market Analysis and Strategy Development," *Journal of Health Care Marketing*, Vol. 10, No. 3, (September, 1990) pp. 12-22.

13. *Ibid.*, p. 13.

14. *Ibid.*

15. *Ibid.*, p. 14.

16. Jeff Goldsmith, "A Radical Prescription for Hospitals," *Harvard Business Review*, May-June, 1989, pp. 104-111.

17. *Ibid.*, p. 105.

18. *Ibid.*, p. 106.

19. *Ibid.*, pp. 107-108.

20. Russell C. Coile, Jr., "Health Care 1990: Outlook for the Decade Ahead," *The New Medicine: Reshaping Medical Practice and Health Care Management,* Aspen, Rockville, MD, 1990, pp. 7-8.

21. *Ibid.,* p. 11.

22. Howard Barich & Philip Kotler, "A Framework for Marketing Image Management," *Sloan Management Review,* Vol. 32, No. 2, Winter, 1991, p. 94 ff.

23. Lisbeth M. Claus, PhD, "Total Quality Management: A Healthcare Application," unpublished, October, 1990.

24. Frank Sabatino, "Priorities? Heart, Cancer, Child/Maternal Care," *Hospitals,* Feb. 20, 1991, pp. 54-55.

25. Taravelia, *op. cit.*

26. Lutz, *op. cit.,* p. 54.

27. Cynthia Wallace, "Centers for Excellence: Humana Hopes to Gain Prestige as Well as More Hospital Inpatients from its Medical Specialty Centers," *Modern Healthcare,* May 20, 1988, p. 30.

28. Berger, *op. cit.*

29. Gerald R. Peters, "Integrated Delivery Can Ally Physician and Hospital Plans," *Healthcare Financial Management,* December, 1991, p. 22.

30. Wheelen & Hunger, *op cit.,* pp. 148-149.

31. *Ibid.*

Chapter 5

MSR in Practice

MSR CASES

This chapter demonstrates when the MSR approach should be used in actual situations and what often happens when it is not applied. The health care facilities are real, as are the situations. However, they have been disguised for obvious reasons.

Consider, for example: St. Mark's Community Hospital, a 450-bed acute care hospital, determined to discontinue its closed psychiatric unit.[1] At the same time, Epsom Memorial Hospital, a 210-bed acute care facility three miles from St. Mark's was considering expanding its psychiatric service. It had a closed unit with excess capacity, and wanted to develop an open unit to offer a full-spectrum of service. Epsom's administration had determined that their closed unit was not attracting patients because there was no flexibility in the treatment modality. Occupancy was frozen at about 15 patients per day in a 30-patient unit.

St. Mark's initially decided to close their unit very rapidly. The decision was made over a weekend. Staff and patients were given notice on Monday that the unit would close on the following Wednesday. Family members, patients, and staff protested to the extent that the closure was delayed for two weeks.

The decision maker looked at the service from a financial point of view as a failing service line. No attempt was made to include the other MSR component: the market analysis. None of the hospital's publics were consulted. Patients and their families first learned of the decision after the fact. Employees and medical staff members were informed at the same time while other programs were contacted only for patient transfers.

St. Mark's received a great deal of adverse publicity. At no time was Epsom Memorial consulted. The unit was closed. Some patients did transfer to Epsom Memorial. However, the dislocation of a fragile population was severe. Research, community input and planning, based on these two, could have helped avoid a black eye for St. Mark's.

Gillete General was a hospital with 155 beds in an older, isolated, blue collar community. Many families' children had grown up and moved away. Despite growing young families in nearby communities, Gillete General experienced a decline in its obstetrical service (from about 500 births per year to around 150). No new obstetricians had joined the staff during this period.

Gillete General had marketed a "Global" package for a routine delivery with little success. A full analysis determined that loss of the obstetrical service would drastically reduce pediatric admissions and impact the emergency service as well. The medical staff agreed that changes had to be made since the service was losing money. Community Advisory Board meetings were helpful.

A capital gift campaign brought in sufficient funds to refurbish the unit and reconfigure it. The unit was able to continue to serve the community.

Barnes Medical Center, a 240-bed acute facility with a 35-bed skilled nursing unit, had a different problem. They considered their physical therapy service to be a cost center instead of a revenue center. Because about 80 percent of their patients were covered by managed care contracts, revenue was not allocated while expenses were. Since the managed care contracts paid on a *per diem* or global fee basis, revenue was not allocated to specific departments.

Equipment was allowed to deteriorate. A study was conducted to determine what alternatives were available. However, this study was based on the financial assumptions stated above. Two years passed. A new study, by the author Dr. Goldman, revealed that it was necessary to develop strict controls for inpatient physical therapy. There was also an opportunity to expand outpatient physical therapy, develop an industrial medicine service, and increase revenues by $350,000 per year.

The estimated cost for upgrading equipment was $75,000. We estimated that the new service would break even in six months because of unique market conditions. The start-up costs were less than $100,000. As with the previous study, no decision was made. The thought of initiating a new program appeared to be radical to an administration faced with the downsizing mentality.

Not all such situations are disasters. Doctors Hospital, a for-profit 105-bed hospital had been in serious financial trouble. Previously, it had been owned by a not-for-profit corporation which lacked sound managerial talent. The administrator had come up through the ranks at the hospital and had started as an accounting clerk. While this future CEO had much experience at this one hospital and was well liked by everyone, there had been no time to acquire either outside experience or a formal education. This person knew of these shortcomings and was hesitant to make decisions that would change a system that everyone was familiar with.

Most of the remainder of the administrative staff had also come up through the ranks in an organization that prided itself on promotion from within. The marketing person was restricted to a few public relations activities while new approaches were looked at with suspicion. The medical staff was very conservative in its approach to managed care. The largest group consisted of four internists and multi-specialty group practice was looked at with suspicion. It was also difficult for new doctors to break in unless sponsored by a retiring physician. Because of these factors, the medical staff was aging and was perceived to be behind the times both clinically and with respect to managed care.

While the hospital had prospered for several years, recently there had been a decline in admissions and procedures to the point that drastic steps needed to be taken.

The medical staff finally came to the conclusion that a new management approach was needed and sought a partner that could infuse needed capital and bring in up-to-date management. The new owners, a for-profit hospital corporation, developed a limited partnership in which the community physicians participated. The physician-partners were shown the hospital's financial statements and projections and learned to understand the business side of hospital management. For example, they reviewed diagnostic procedures to find ways to cut costs without affecting quality. They rapidly became true partners in managing Doctors Hospital. Today, this hospital is providing excellent care to its community and is operating at a profit. The MSR technique was successfully applied at Doctors because both the objectives and the management structure were modified.

Wilde Memorial is a 200-bed acute care hospital in a wealthy suburban area with several direct competitors and a population base of about three million. A few years ago, Wilde's administration was looking for a new center of excellence with the objectives of increasing net revenue and filling unused space.

Their choice was an alcohol and substance abuse inpatient program for teenagers. Instead of developing a joint venture with a successful substance abuse vendor, Wilde developed its own program. The inpatient length of stay was 45 days, about 15 to 20 days longer than the typical program and the price was $15,000 for the complete program.

The program included some outpatient counseling and small group intervention in addition to the inpatient segment. It lost money every year. After four years of major financial support with little growth and a minimal level of interest by community providers, a decision was made to eliminate the program. However, Wilde's administration chose to harvest rather than divest.

A search was initiated to find a new home for the program with no success. That is, no hospital within a reasonable distance was willing to take over the program with its losing track record. To overcome this problem, an alternate method was attempted.

The community, through a series of radio and local print ads, was asked to help find a new home for the program. As an option, community groups could agree to sponsor the program and keep it at Wilde. Neither option proved to be popular and the program was phased out.

An MSR approach would have turned up the following problems:

1. Wilde's administration had no expertise in developing and marketing this type of program.
2. The product was inappropriate. While the longer inpatient stay was considered an advantage by the administration, patients and third-party payors found the cost to be an obstacle.
3. Provider support could not be developed. (It is unclear if this is because of the poor product or a lack on the part of Wilde's staff.)
4. The community did not want to continue the program under the two options offered by the hospital and presented to them.

It would probably be safe to say that an MSR analysis before the program was started would have raised severe doubts about progressing. Even if an MSR approach had been taken as late as when the harvest decision was made, the situation might have been less costly. The community was given options instead of being asked for input.

This approach precluded a buy-in by the community and cut off discussion on fresh alternatives. While the program might not have been saved at this stage in its life cycle, we will never know what could have been done.

AN MSR DISASTER

One case combines practically all potential mistakes in one situation. The case is followed by an analysis of what happened.

DeAnza Community Hospital is located in the San Francisco Bay Area, and is a prestigious acute care hospital of 510 beds in a market with ten competitors. Occupancy rate was stalled at about 55 percent. Several hospitals had closed or merged in the last few years.

The marketing staff included a Director of Public Relations, with a journalism background, and a Director of Contracting with a background of employment with a major health maintenance organization.

Looking at the success of other hospitals, the senior administrative staff attempted to develop several "Centers of Excellence," a valid marketing strategy. A community-based hospital, with a reasonable market share and stiff competition, attempts to develop new business by reaching out beyond its primary market with a specialized service. The goal is to have patients seek out the hospital because of the excellent reputation and facilities associated with the service.

DeAnza's Chief Executive Officer Joe Fisher and Chief Financial Officer Ellen Anderson, chose a sub-specialty service that required a population of over 1.5 million to support it. This was acceptable in a region of about five million people. However, two competitors were already established.

One competing service was located at a local medical school. The other, at Alzheimer Memorial, the largest private hospital in the area: a hospital with an excellent reputation and a major share of the market.

Dr. Harold Thomas had an established practice and a clinical teaching position at the local medical school. Dr. Thomas was well respected and had been involved in the training of many of the sub-specialists currently in practice.

Fisher and Anderson approached Dr. Thomas to suggest that the doctor's practice relocate to DeAnza. An office and clinic were created. Dr. Thomas's specifications were reasonable, but exacting. The hospital maintenance personnel made several errors in construction. For example: equipment shelves were too small.

Since Dr. Thomas's practice was dependent upon referrals from specialists, Drs. Queen, Fisher, and Anderson agreed that two other physicians would be recruited to share the space provided by DeAnza. With Dr. Thomas's help two qualified specialists were recruited. They had both trained under Dr. Thomas whom they respected. At the last minute, they were given space in a medical office building owned by the hospital.

A conflict had developed. Several medical staff members heard about the new practice through the informal network. They objected to the placement of two referring physicians with a competitor. Fisher felt threatened by this situation. Thus the last minute switch.

Referrals to Dr. Thomas decreased markedly. Instead of the projected 20 patients per week, Dr. Thomas was seeing about five per week. About 60 percent of the patients seen did not need Dr. Thomas's highly specialized procedures. While they generated revenue, they did not require the specialized technology of Dr. Thomas's practice.

Dr. Thomas and the hospital administration agreed to the development of a promotional piece. About $10,000 was spent on design and printing of a run of 5,000 of these promotional folders. The piece consisted of a slick two-color folder with pockets. One pocket had a Rolodex cut out, the other held a business card for Dr. Thomas. The Rolodex card did not have an upper tab for easy location. The piece contained several information sheets that explained the services offered.

The folder was able to hold standard paper without folds. However, it could not fit into a full-sized business envelope. The administration determined that this would have added to the price of the piece. The use of the brochure is not clear to the authors. We understand that a direct mail campaign was not planned. Presumably, the piece was to be used to respond to inquiries: something a less expensive item could accomplish. No small brochure, designed to fit in a Number 10 envelope was designed.

Dr. Thomas expected to generate income by having a small dispensing retail operation within the office complex. This store would sell the medical equipment and supplies associated with the practice.[2] While the space was developed and furnished, operations were delayed. Dr. Thomas attempted to obtain permission to begin retail sales. No decision was forthcoming. Time passed and expenses increased.

Anderson left DeAnza. The New Chief Financial Officer, Chris Macauley, was told that Dr. Thomas was difficult to get along with. Since the financial picture was dismal, Macauley recommended that expenses be cut.

At this point, the total investment by DeAnza was over $500,000 in opportunity costs for the space, renovation costs, the promotional piece, and a salary for Dr. Thomas. This physician had used a second mortgage on the family residence in the amount of $250,000 to invest in the project.

Susan Bankowsky, an attorney, was asked to mediate the situation. An attempt to reestablish the spirit of cooperation that was originally present failed. Expenses mounted with no progress. One of the authors (Goldman) was also brought in with the same results.

Dr. Thomas was informed by Macauley that the partnership would be terminated in three months unless revenue increased.

Dr. Thomas restated requests to open the retail operation and to bring in two referral physicians. Neither Fisher nor Macauley responded.

Lawsuits have been filed and the unit is no longer providing service. Valuable equipment is idle and a staff of well-trained technicians have moved on to other jobs. Could this disaster have been turned around? Perhaps.

In this case, managerial indecision and a lack of planning on the part of Fisher and Anderson resulted in stunting the life cycle of the sub-specialty service. A Question Mark (high growth potential) was turned into a Dog. At several points the MSR technique could have been applied. The authors believe that DeAnza and Dr. Thomas could have succeeded if it had been applied.

MSR APPLICATION POINTS
IN THE DEANZA/THOMAS CASE

1. Fisher and Anderson failed to consider the needs of the existing medical staff. When the other specialists did hear about the project, it was in a manner that would ensure their opposition. They had the political clout that Dr. Thomas lacked.

The hospital administration could have laid the groundwork for a successful service by engaging in basic marketing research. They would have been able to analyze their competitors and the concerns of their medical staff.

2. No thought was given to the existing programs and their response to competition from the new program. While there was room for two programs, establishment of a third program would have required extraordinary efforts to capture market share. In addition, the market was in the maturity stage with few new families moving into the immediate area of DeAnza. An early Go No-Go decision would have been reasonable.

3. The initial budget was too small, given the change in referrals that developed. The promotional piece was beautiful but far

too costly. It was poorly designed as well. By developing a marketing plan, all elements, including the promotional materials, would have been coordinated.

4. Facility design and location of the office and clinic added to the problems. The space was difficult to find and did not meet Dr. Thomas' needs. Factoring this limitation into the plan would have had a strong impact on the decision whether to proceed.

5. The change in Chief Financial Officers increased the speed of decline. The new Chief Financial Officer, Macauley, had little interest and no commitment to the project. Fisher had lost interest and even felt threatened by Dr. Thomas and the backlash from the other physicians.

A thorough review of the project was in order. Dr. Thomas and Macauley should have met with the other concerned physicians to settle disputes and restructure the services.

6. No effort was made to restructure the service. De facto changes were made without planning or consultation with Dr. Thomas.

7. The hospital ignored the advice of its legal and marketing consultants.

8. Perhaps the single most important cause for the failure was the lack of a competent project manager with responsibility for the project.

9. DeAnza assumed that Dr. Thomas's service was a Dog. The assumption was self-fulfilling.

AN MSR SUCCESS WHERE OTHERS FAILED

A few years after St. Mark's and Epsom attempted to restructure mental health services with little success, Luce Memorial faced a similar situation. While inpatient mental health services comprised about 20 percent of revenues, expenses were high so that the unit was providing only a small contribution to overhead, the physician base had eroded, and morale on the unit was very low. This was attributed to the increased market share of managed care plans in the area which restricted access to mental health services as a cost containment measure. (Note: patient demand for these services had not decreased.)

The MSR analysis included a review of four alternatives that had been proposed to management.

1. Elimination of the service. Without a replacement of revenue, Luce Memorial would see a worsening in its financial position.

2. Rebuild and augment the service through intensive program development and physician recruiting. Since there were several strong competitors sharing the market with Luce, this was seen as a difficult choice to implement.

3. Negotiate a contract with a nonprofit organization that had broad experience in managing mental health units. This organization had broad experience in the managed care arena that Luce Memorial was competing in. However, it appeared that it would take this organization more time than could be allocated to the project.

4. Contract with a for-profit management firm that had a proven track record of rapid turnaround of mental health units, but no experience with managed care.

Each alternative appeared to be unacceptable. Without a complete MSR analysis, the least bad might have been chosen. That could have been the unstated option of maintaining the *status quo*. All too often, this is the route of administrators who fear making a decision that could be detrimental to their careers.

In this situation, an outside consultant and senior management developed an approach that was comprehensive in nature. It met the hospital's need to maintain revenue while improving quality and morale. It also met the needs of the community for both inpatient and out-patient mental health services.

A consortium of mental health providers was developed. It included for-profit units within non-profit hospitals, out-patient services provided by the county Department of Health Services and private providers.

Luce Memorial curtailed the marketing of its inpatient unit while accepting patients from several groups in the area that had specific needs that Luce was best capable of meeting. Luce also agreed to participate in multi-organizational ambulatory programs that improved the provision of mental health services to Medicaid recipients and were well received by several managed care organizations.

Luce Memorial's approach was bold, decisive, and complete. Services were properly analyzed. The four alternatives that were a poor fit as well as the do-nothing approach were all rejected and replaced with cooperation with other providers. The needs of the community were met while Luce Memorial lost little net revenue.

CONCLUSIONS

Even by BCG criteria, a "Dog" could be continued so long as it shows some profit. However, the MSR strategy suggests that a proper analysis of profit or loss of a service requires that expenses and revenues be meticulously isolated. This is essential because a decline in demand of one service may affect the demand of another related service.[3]

The MSR strategy requires an examination of alternate restructuring options including realignment, increased promotion, managed divestiture and community involvement before a service termination. Restructuring can lead to future expansion and profitability.

Moreover, the extended life of a service allows managers time to analyze relevant future trends in the light of the changing economic and social environment. A continued service also improves the public image of the organization.

As managed care moves into the next phase, the IDS/MSO

model–the type of analysis used in the MSR approach–will become increasingly more important. Competition, particularly managed competition, will mandate that each SBU will contribute to the overall mission as well as advance the financial objectives of the organization. One view of managed care is that it is an implementation of the MSR approach.

Centers of excellence will continue to be an important marketing tool. To give these centers every opportunity to succeed, they will need objective and accurate analytical support as well as commitment by senior and mid-level management.

We conclude that in any situation involving service reconsideration, the MSR strategy is a viable alternative to immediate elimination of the service. Both the financial and the marketing aspects must be analyzed and the two disciplines integrated.

REFERENCE NOTES

1. Goldman & Schore, *Healthcare, op. cit.*, p. 12.

2. This is a common practice. For example, ophthalmologists often co-locate with dispensing opticians and otorhinolaryngologists sometimes have a hearing aid dispenser on the premises.

3. Goldman & Mukherjee, *op cit.*

Index